CANDIED

A Comedy Drama in Three Acts

by

FALKLAND L. CARY

SAMUEL  FRENCH

LONDON

NEW YORK TORONTO SYDNEY HOLLYWOOD

ISBN978-0-573-01061-3

www.samuelfrench.co.uk
www.samuelfrench.com

TO

ALEX REEVE

Producer, Northampton Repertory Company,

in gratitude and admiration.

CANDIED PEEL

Presented on December 4th, 1944, by the Northampton Repertory Players with the following cast of characters:

(*In order of their appearance*)

James Ondersley	*Peter Tremlett*
Lucy French	*Peggy Diamond*
Mrs Seddons	*Mary Russell*
Grace Lenner	*Mary Whitfield*
Henrietta	*Doreen Markham*
Miss Pethington	*Margaret Pepler*
Dr Wadd	*Lawrence Baskcomb*
Claire Brisby	*Pauline Williams*
Leonard Brisby	*Arthur R. Webb*
Oswald Monk	*John Falconer*
Mrs Corntonhart	*Dorothy Fenwick*
Mr Harris	*Reginald Thorne*

Settings designed by Osborne Robinson
The Play produced by Alex Reeve

SYNOPSIS OF SCENES.

Scene: James Ondersley's Drawing-room

ACT I

Scene 1 Before Dinner.

Scene 2. After Breakfast next morning.

ACT II

Scene 1. Before Dinner the same day.

Scene 2. The same, five minutes later.

ACT III

After Dinner, the same evening.

Time: The Autumn.

Note. It is of advantage if the characters can wear evening dress in Act I Scene 1, Act II and Act III, but it is not essential.

CANDIED PEEL

ACT I.

SCENE 1.

SCENE—MR JAMES ONDERSLEY'S *drawing-room about seven o'clock in the evening. It is pleasantly and modernly furnished in bright and attractive colours. The sort of room you would expect to see where neither taste, nor the means to gratify it, was missing. There is nothing whatever stiff or formal about it. One is not intimidated by values, not made resentful by prices. Altogether the room of a man or woman to whom a pleasing room is an essential and presents no difficulty.*

There is a door well down stage R., *and another up stage rather* R. *of the* C. *The fireplace is* L.C. *In front of the fireplace, and at right angles to it, is a long settee behind which there is a table (used for drinks). On the table is a telephone.*

In front of the fire is a stool, and still further down stage, an easy chair with its back to the audience. There is a pouffe down stage C.

An armchair is half-way down stage R.C., *with a small table behind it, on which is a vase of flowers and a box of candied peel. (Note that the box should be bright and distinctive.)*

There is a small chair below the door down R. *Also a small radio on the stage* R., *above the door down* R. *It is playing as the curtain rises.*

(*See the Ground plan at the end of the play.*)

MR ONDERSLEY *is a figure of some distinction. His age might be forty, or even five years older. Not the sort of man one would pass in the street without being tempted to look round after him. There is nothing sinister or strange in his appearance, but the distinction is there, all right. Something about the carriage of his head, the incisive walk, the forceful economy of gesture, conveys it. He has a pleasing voice, as pleasing as the owner's personality. Perhaps hair that is graying at the temples adds to that distinction of his.*

The world amuses him considerably; so considerably that he is careful not to show it and his most outrageous remarks are made without a smile.

His cynicism may appear complete, but it is likeable; as likeable as the man himself. He enjoys his wealth, takes it almost for granted, perhaps, but he has never allowed it to spoil him.

At the moment he is standing by the fireplace, contemplatively smoking a cigarette. Almost immediately after the curtain rises he walks across to the table on which the box of candied peel is lying, puts his cigarette on the ashtray there, crushing it out as he does so. Then he takes up the box of candied peel and sniffs it carefully, selects a small piece and puts it in his mouth. He then goes to the radio R. *and switches it off as* LUCY FRENCH *enters, up* C.

She is his London secretary. A girl of twenty-six or seven; business-like, but quite at home in her surroundings and, obviously, a person of some intelligence.

She comes to his left just above the armchair R.C.

LUCY (*handing* ONDERSLEY *two or three letters*). These are ready, Mr Ondersley, if you will sign them.

(ONDERSLEY *moves to the armchair and sits,* LUCY *gets a book lying on the settee for him to rest the paper on which he signs.*)

ONDERSLEY. I must be the world's most inconsiderate employer. I ask my secretary to spend her week-end acting hostess for me; and then dictate letters to her.

LUCY (*laughing*). They didn't take five minutes.

(LUCY *crosses to the armchair down* L. *sits and puts the letters in the envelopes.* MRS SEDDONS *enters* R. *with a decanter containing sherry on a tray.* MRS SEDDONS *is a pleasant person. She entirely fails to understand* ONDERSLEY, *but mothers him indefatigably. She puts down the decanter on the table behind the settee.*)

ONDERSLEY (*rises and moves up to* MRS SEDDONS' R.). Ah, the sherry, Mrs Seddons?

Mrs Seddons. Yes, Mr Ondersley, I've brought....

(ONDERSLEY *interrupts her with a quick gesture and, taking the stopper out of the decanter, sniffs the sherry with appreciation.*)

ONDERSLEY. The Amontillado, labelled 1880.

MRS SEDDONS. Yes, sir, that's right. (*She is genuinely impressed.*) I've seen you do that a dozen times with different bottles of sherry, and you've never guessed wrong.

ONDERSLEY. Guessed! My sense of smell tells me one sherry from another as easily as you tell a good egg from a bad one. (*Reflectively.*) And one comes across a few bad 'uns....(*He crosses to the table above the easy chair.*)

MRS SEDDONS (*taking him literally*). I wouldn't say that, sir. Nearly all the eggs I open are good.

ONDERSLEY. That's because their mothers were hens, not women. (*He takes another piece of candied peel.*)

MRS SEDDONS (*going towards the door* R.). If you'll excuse my saying it, sir, eating all that candied peel couldn't be good for you.
ONDERSLEY (*suddenly serious*). You're right, Mrs Seddons. It couldn't be good for me, and it might be extremely bad.

(GRACE LENNER *enters* R. *She is* ONDERSLEY'S *ward until she is twenty-five, and has two years to go to that date. She is an extremely good-looking girl, with charming easy manners.*)

GRACE (*just inside the door*). Hello, J.O. Hello, Lucy.

(*Exit* MRS SEDDONS, *closing the door.*)

ONDERSLEY (*crossing to the front of the settee, without looking at* GRACE). Nice ward I've got, haven't I, Miss French, deserting my week-end party and running off to her own friends?

(GRACE *goes to the* R. *of the settee.*)

LUCY (*smiling*). It's a first offence, Mr Ondersley.
ONDERSLEY. First offence, indeed! She hasn't had time to do it before. Damn it, she only came back from Scotland last week.
GRACE (*sitting on the* R. *arm of the settee*). And who are your week-enders, anyway? Anyone interesting, Lucy?
LUCY. Dr Wadd.
GRACE. Very nice, but I shouldn't say very interesting.
LUCY. Mrs Corntonhart.
ONDERSLEY. Very interesting—but I shouldn't say very nice.
GRACE. What an extraordinary name. Who is she?
ONDERSLEY. An old....(*he pauses*) friend of mine.
GRACE. Oh, one of those?
ONDERSLEY (*indignantly*). Not one of those at all.
GRACE. Well, who else?
LUCY. Mr and Mrs Brisby.
GRACE. I like Claire Brisby. (*To* ONDERSLEY *accusingly.*) So do you. Thou shalt not covet thy partner's wife....and I dislike your partner, Mr Brisby. Quite a lot. Is that the whole boiling?
ONDERSLEY. That, is the whole boiling!
LUCY. Except Mr Monk.
GRACE (*quickly*). Oswald Monk. (*To* LUCY.) Well, I'm glad there's *something* for you.
LUCY. Don't be absurd. (*But the shot is not altogether wide.*)
GRACE. Have you taken on that invention of his yet?
ONDERSLEY. No. It wouldn't have helped us.
GRACE. I expect you're wrong. What did Mr. Brisby think?
ONDERSLEY. He thought it might. Must say the experts rather backed the idea.
GRACE. He was right, and you got your way. Typical procedure in the firm of Ondersley.

ONDERSLEY (*moving level with her*). Look here, young woman. Only one person is allowed to make decisions in the firm over my head. (*With a nod at* LUCY.) My secretary. I can't stop her.
GRACE (*undaunted*). I wouldn't stand it, Lucy. Why don't you get yourself transferred to the Scottish Branch?
LUCY. Thanks for the suggestion. (*She rises.*) I'll just get these letters off. (*She goes to the door up* C.)
ONDERSLEY. Don't be long. The party will descend upon me shortly.
LUCY. I'll be back in a minute or two.

(*She goes out up* C.)

GRACE (*rising and getting a cigarette from the table behind the settee*). By the way, Miss Pethington's waiting to see you.
ONDERSLEY (*crossing and lighting* GRACE'S *cigarette*). Who, and why is Miss Pethington?
GRACE. One of *your* numerous admirers. She's the Village Institution. I think she's a little mad....but quite nice.
ONDERSLEY (*moving downstage and going towards the fireplace*). May I ask what this lady wants with me?
GRACE. Money, I imagine.
ONDERSLEY. What for?
GRACE. I haven't the faintest idea. She wasn't very clear (*with a smile*) but I told her you'd give her a cheque.
ONDERSLEY. Thank you, Grace, thank you....That was extremely generous of *you.*
GRACE (*moving to the settee and sitting*). Well, you always do.
ONDERSLEY. Why did you tell this miserable woman to call now? I wanted a few minutes with you before you went. I won't see her.

(HENRIETTA, *a smart-looking maid, comes in* R. *with some sherry glasses on a tray, as they are speaking. She puts the tray on the table behind the settee.*)

GRACE. Henrietta, Mr Ondersley will see Miss Pethington now.
HENRIETTA. Yes, Miss Grace. (*She starts to move* R.)
ONDERSLEY. Henrietta, Mr Ondersley will not.
HENRIETTA. No, Mr Ondersley. (*She turns back again.*)
GRACE. Of course you will.
ONDERSLEY (*with a gesture of fury*). Henrietta, do what the master of this house tells you.
HENRIETTA. Yes, Mr, Ondersley. (*She goes* R. *again.*)
ONDERSLEY. I mean, show Miss Pethington in.
HENRIETTA. That's what I was going to do, sir.
ONDERSLEY (*with a gesture of despair*). All right, Henrietta. Show Miss Pethington in....in five minutes' time.
HENRIETTA. Very good, sir.

(*She goes out* R. ONDERSLEY *laughs and strolls across to the candied peel, and picks a piece up.*)

GRACE. You'll spoil your appetite.

(ONDERSLEY *pauses, looks at the candied peel, pauses again, and puts it in his mouth. He then crosses to the end of settee and sits.*)

GRACE. Dear J.O. It really was nice of you to fix up the week-end for me. . . I believe you want to get rid of me !
ONDERSLEY. You'll enjoy being at the Williamson's more than running this party.
GRACE. Sure I will.
ONDERSLEY. Splendid, when are you coming back to me ?
GRACE. Tuesday morning.
ONDERSLEY. It's an eternity. Hang it ! You're only just back from three months in Scotland.
GRACE. Don't be absurd, J.O. But it's sweet of you to let me go.
ONDERSLEY. Sweet....it's damned unselfish. (*He turns away.*)
GRACE. Unselfish ?
ONDERSLEY. Giving up something I want....very much.
GRACE. You do love to dramatise yourself, don't you ?
ONDERSLEY. If you can't be affectionate, young woman, you should at least be respectful.
GRACE. I'll be respectfulness itself.
ONDERSLEY. If your uncle hadn't asked me to....
GRACE. To act as guardian to his poverty-stricken little niece. Well, what.... ?
ONDERSLEY (*suddenly*). How old are you ?
GRACE. Twenty-three.
ONDERSLEY. And I'm forty-five....That's what....
GRACE. What's your income, J.O. ?
ONDERSLEY. I don't know....exactly.
GRACE. Some thousands ?
ONDERSLEY. I suppose so.
GRACE. And mine will be a hundred-and-fifty a year. That's what....
ONDERSLEY. I don't see it's got anything to do with it.... Grace.... (*He moves nearer to her.*) I know there are all sorts of difficulties.... and differences....Age....I'm forty-five....you're twenty-three... Does that make....it utterly impossible ?
GRACE. Am I to be respectful....or affectionate, now ?
ONDERSLEY. If it's got to be only one..... affectionate..... definitely....
GRACE. If....
ONDERSLEY (*eagerly*). Yes ?
GRACE. If we did....if we did get married....you know what everybody'd say.
ONDERSLEY. That you were throwing yourself away on an old man.

GRACE. That I had married the Ondersley fortune.
ONDERSLEY. What the hell does it matter what they say, provided....?
GRACE. Provided....?
ONDERSLEY. We love each other.
GRACE. I wonder....?
ONDERSLEY. Damn it (*he rises and crosses towards the stool* L.)....this is ridiculous. I'm behaving like a schoolboy.
GRACE. You are.
ONDERSLEY. Tell me one thing, Grace. Is there someone else in the picture?
GRACE (*after a slight hesitation*). No.
ONDERSLEY. Doesn't sound too convincing, that negative. There is....
GRACE (*with less hesitation*). No.
ONDERSLEY. There was, though.

(GRACE *nods.*)

That's something. Is he dead? I hope he is.
GRACE. That's perfectly horrid of you.
ONDERSLEY. Someone you met in Scotland?

(GRACE *nods again.*)

Well, you've had a lucky escape. All the Scotch are bigamists.
GRACE. They'd like to hear you say that, wouldn't they?
ONDERSLEY. It wouldn't worry them. Scotsmen find it cheaper to be kept by two women instead of one. Who was he? Thank God it's the past tense.
GRACE. I'm not going to tell you, J.O. (*She rises.*) It's all over, anyway, and that five minutes must be up now.
ONDERSLEY. Not at all; Henrietta's a tactful girl.

(*The door opens* R. *and* HENRIETTA *comes in.*)

Damn her....she isn't.
HENRIETTA. Miss Pethington, sir.

(HENRIETTA *opens the door for* MISS PETHINGTON, *and that lady enters.* MISS PETHINGTON *is about fifty and is given to lost causes. In the harmony of life she is, indeed, herself a lost chord. But that does not prevent her being indefatigable in her support of whatever may be the standard under which she is marching. She is vague to a degree and finds it hard to choose the exact word to express her meaning, without trying others first. Once chosen, however, she sticks to her word with surprising emphasis.* GRACE *moves to greet her as she comes in.* HENRIETTA *exits* R.)

GRACE. Good evening, Miss Pethington. You've come at the right moment. You'll find my guardian in his most amiable mood just before dinner.

(*In the ensuing dialogue*, GRACE *moves well down stage* L. *to armchair, and watches* ONDERSLEY *attempting to deal with* MISS PETHINGTON, *with no little amusement.*)

ONDERSLEY (*going to meet her*). How do you do, Miss Pethington ?

MISS PETHINGTON. How do you do, Mr Ondersley ? So very kind of you to see me.

ONDERSLEY (*politely*). Not at all. (*He waits for her to continue.*) Do sit down.

(*She sits down on the* R. *of the settee.*)

Well....? (*He sits on her* L.)

(GRACE *sits in the armchair down* L.)

MISS PETHINGTON (*taking him up instantly*). Very well indeed. And yourself, too, I hope. (*In a rush.*) What a wonderful autumn we *ought* to be having, oughtn't we ?

ONDERSLEY. Yes....yes. I suppose we autumned....ought, I mean. (*After a pause.*) I hope you didn't get wet on the way here.

MISS PETHINGTON. Wet. Oh, no. Perhaps a little damp, perhaps.... but not *wet*....(*She smiles to herself.*)

ONDERSLEY. That's good. (*He again waits for her to speak, and looks helplessly at* GRACE, *who makes no effort to assist.*)

MISS PETHINGTON. I took a little liberty....a short cut through your fruit garden....the strawberry garden....

ONDERSLEY. I'm afraid the strawberries weren't very good this year. The wet weather, so the gardener tells me, and the slugs.

MISS PETHINGTON. The slugs....slugs !....I don't really dislike slugs. (*Thinks a little vaguely.*) And....you don't have to think about the bones, do you ?

ONDERSLEY (*firmly taking the situation in hand*). No. No. But I'm sure you haven't come here to talk to me about slugs....

MISS PETHINGTON (*waving away the suggestion*). Of course....not about slugs....but about (*firmly*) the Village Eugenics Society.

ONDERSLEY. The Village what Society ?

MISS PETHINGTON. Eugenics. The application of the laws of heredity to the improvement of the human race. (*She has managed that definition quite safely, and looks delighted about it.*)

ONDERSLEY (*surprised*). But do you really think there's need for Eugenics in this little garden of a village ?

MISS PETHINGTON (*with surprising fluency and conviction, and rising as she speaks*). Ah ! What a different place the world would be if only Adam and Eve had possessed a knowledge of Eugenics in *their* little garden.

ONDERSLEY (*completely floored*). How right you are ! (*He rises and crosses to the table behind the easy chair.*)

(GRACE *watches his discomfiture with considerable pleasure.*)

(*He automatically puts his hand on the candied peel box, and then, recollects himself.*) Have a cocktail, Miss Pethington ?

(MISS PETHINGTON *shakes her head.*)

Or a piece of candied peel ? (*He brings the box towards her.*)

MISS PETHINGTON. Candied peel....Delicious. (*She is about to take a piece, then apparently changes her mind.*) No thank you.

ONDERSLEY (*returning to the table*). You were saying that a knowledge of Eugenics....(*He pauses.*)

MISS PETHINGTON (*firmly*). The villagers must learn the principles of heredity, if they are to breed healthy children.

ONDERSLEY. I should have thought the last thing in the world *these* villagers needed to be taught was how to breed. They seem to know it all too well. However, as you are an authority on breeding....

MISS PETHINGTON (*shocked*). Oh, no, no. (*Hastily.*) On Eugenics, on Eugenics. You must not misunderstand me.

ONDERSLEY (*he is now edging her towards the door*). Well....I shall be delighted to send you a cheque. Or perhaps you'll call for it if I leave it for you.

MISS PETHINGTON. But that is generous....municipal....munificent. ....That is very generous of you.

(*To his horror she makes a little run to the settee, and sits down again.*)

And now, *now*....you'd like to hear all about our plans.

(DR WADD *enters, up* C. *He is an elderly man—about sixty, perhaps, outspoken in manner, and a complete foil to* ONDERSLEY ; *which is, possibly the reason why the two men like each other.* GRACE *rises.*)

ONDERSLEY (*as* WADD *comes in*). You must be a regular thought-reader ! (*Firmly.*) But here's Dr Wadd coming to rescue....interrupt us. (*He is now standing by the down stage edge of the easy chair facing* MISS PETHINGTON.)

WADD. Evening, Ondersley.

ONDERSLEY. Wadd, I'm sure you know Miss Pethington. (*He moves to the* R. *of* WADD *near the door bringing him down to* MISS PETHINGTON.)

DR WADD. Of course I do. How are you, Miss Pethington ? Evening, Grace. Are you going or coming ? (*He crosses* L. *to the fireplace.*)

GRACE (*moving to the* R. *centre*). Going. I'm taking your own prescription. A couple of days at the sea.

MISS PETHINGTON (*rising*). Ah....the sea....those wonderful days by the side of the sea. (*She smiles coyly.*) And I don't mind making a guess, Miss Lenner, that when no one's looking....you'll.... you'll (*daringly*) paddle.

GRACE. Let me drive you down to your house.

MISS PETHINGTON. No, no, please. If one finds one's way in....one finds one's way *out* again. That is....that is (*looking around her doubtfully*) I *hope* so.

ONDERSLEY (*feelingly*). Indeed, I hope so, too.

GRACE. I'll be passing your house. Good-bye, Dr Wadd. (*She moves up to the door* C.)

(ONDERSLEY *waves good-bye to her.*)

DR WADD. Come along, Miss Pethington. (*He goes towards her.*)

MISS PETHINGTON (*to* ONDERSLEY). Good-bye, Mr Ondersley. Thank you so much. I knew you would sympathise. Sympathise as a man and a father. But then (*she is getting confused*)....of course.... you're a bachelor....so you can't be a father.... or can you ....? Dear me....dear me.... it's all very confusing. isn't it ?

(*She talks herself out* R.)

GRACE (*at the door*). Can you....or can't you....? Good-bye, J.O.

(GRACE *exits* R.)

DR WADD (*laughing*). Your sins seem to be finding you out !

ONDERSLEY. Your Miss Pethington's quite mad, of course. (*He crosses to the drinks table.*)

DR WADD (*moving to the stool* L. *and sitting*). Forty years of general practice have convinced me that everyone has a sane place, somewhere. Even you, J.O. Though it doesn't stick out.

ONDERSLEY (*with a smile*). Have some candied peel with your sherry ? (*He pours out the sherry without waiting for a reply.*)

DR WADD. No, thanks. There's one thing about you, Ondersley, your sherry's always good.

ONDERSLEY. *And* my morals, don't forget them. (*He crosses with the sherry to* DR WADD *then goes back for his own drink.*)

DR WADD. I can swallow your sherry....What was Miss Pethington bothering you about ?

ONDERSLEY (*sitting on the* R. *arm of the settee*). Wanted a subscription. Damn it, man, you ought to know all about it. Birth Control or something.

DR WADD. Eugenics, my lad, that's what you're thinking of. Eugenics. Taking thought for to-morrow.

ONDERSLEY. Well, isn't that Birth Control ? (*He drinks.*)

DR WADD. No, Birth Control is taking *care* for to-morrow.

ONDERSLEY. But what would a stainless bachelor like me know about such a thing ?

DR WADD. Everything fixed up for this extra-ordinary dinner party of yours ?

ONDERSLEY. Yes. (*He rises and puts down his glass on the table.*) The feast is set, the guests are met, and—

(*as* LEONARD BRISBY *and his wife* CLAIRE *come in*)

—they're already entering in.

(HENRIETTA *enters* R.)

HENRIETTA. Mr and Mrs Brisby.

(WADD *rises and puts his glass on the mantelpiece.*)

(LEONARD BRISBY *is a partner of* ONDERSLEY'S *and the two men are a complete contrast, for, whilst the latter appears to enjoy life very thoroughly, the former gets very little kick out of it. He is older than* ONDERSLEY, *a rather pompous person, given to the laying down of dogmas, and utterly without humour.* CLAIRE—*why did she marry the man ?—is charming, quite a few years younger than her husband. She dresses well, and is all for a good time. Possibly this accounts for some of* BRISBY'S *unhappiness.* HENRIETTA *exits* R.)

CLAIRE (*coming in*). Hello, J.O. Good evening Dr Wadd.
ONDERSLEY. Charmed to see you, Claire. Evening, Brisby.
DR WADD. How do you do, Mrs Brisby ?

(*These speeches are nearly overlapping.*)

BRISBY. Good evening, Ondersley. (*He crosses to* WADD.) How do you do, Wadd, how do you do ? (*He shakes hand with* WADD *by the up stage end of the stool.*)
CLAIRE. Very sweet of you to ask us down, J.O.
ONDERSLEY (*bringing her to the settee*). Very sweet of you to come, my dear.
CLAIRE. And we're *full* of curiosity. (*She sits on the* L. *end of the settee.*)
ONDERSLEY. Curiosity ? (*He goes to the drinks.*)
CLAIRE. Well....you said it was *most important* we should come.
ONDERSLEY. So it is, for the success of the party.
BRISBY. It's most kind of you to have asked us, Ondersley, but I must point out we were only able to accept your invitation at *considerable inconvenience* to ourselves....I hope the use of the words " most important " was actually justified by the facts.
ONDERSLEY (*interrupting him*). Drown your eloquence in drink, Brisby. What can I get for you, Claire ?
DR WADD. I'd have sherry, Mrs Brisby. You do know what it is.

(ONDERSLEY *pours out one sherry.*)

ONDERSLEY. Whilst what James Ondersley puts into a cocktail is known only to himself and his Maker.

(LUCY *has come in up* C. *as the others are speaking.*)

LUCY (*to* ONDERSLEY). So sorry, Mr Ondersley. The long distance call you wanted has just come through.

ONDERSLEY. It would. I'll take it in the library. Shan't be a moment. Carry on with the....the jug and bottle department, Miss French.

(*He goes out up* C. LUCY *moves to the drinks table.*)

CLAIRE. And how is the world treating Miss French?
LUCY. Much as Miss French treats the world, I suppose. So, so. That right? (*She hands* CLAIRE *a sherry.*)
CLAIRE. Looks wonderful.
LUCY. Mr Brisby?
BRISBY. A little plain gin for me, Miss French. I assume you came here on an " urgent " summons, too.
DR WADD. Can you tell us what other guests are expected?

(LUCY *hands a gin to* BRISBY.)

LUCY. Mr Monk....you know him. Another, Doctor?
DR WADD. Thank you.,

(LUCY *goes back to the table and refills* WADD's *glass.*)

BRISBY. That is very singular. Why should be he invited? You remember, my dear, a young scientist, I mentioned his name to you. He submitted plans of a new process to Ondersley, but my partner rejected it. Very....very....singular. (*He moves down stage to the pouffe.*)

(LUCY *brings the drink to* WADD.)

CLAIRE. Perhaps it's a sort of business dinner....

(HENRIETTA *opens the door* R. *and shows in* MONK.)

BRISBY. No, I think not. You and Dr Wadd are hardly members of the firm.

(MONK *enters after* HENRIETTA. *He is twenty-three or four years old. Unlike* ONDERSLEY, *when he says something amusing he shows that he likes his audience to be aware of it.*)

HENRIETTA. Mr Monk.

(LUCY *turns.* HENRIETTA *exits* R.)

MONK (*at the doorway, seeing* LUCY). Hello....Good evening.... Miss French.
LUCY. How do you do, Mr Monk? (*She crosses* R. *a little.*)

BRISBY. Good evening, Mr Monk. I confess I am quite astonished to meet you here.
MONK. The invitation came as a bit of a surprise, I admit. (*He moves across to the easy chair* R.)
BRISBY. The *urgent* invitation? Was it by any chance, an urgent invitation?

(LUCY *moves to the drinks table.*)

MONK (*looking at him*). Yes....Curiously enough, it was.
BRISBY. You have not met my wife. Claire, may I introduce Mr Monk?
MONK. How do you do, Mrs Brisby?
CLAIRE. How do you do?
BRISBY. And Dr Wadd.
DR WADD. How do you do?
LUCY. Sherry or cocktail, Mr Monk?
MONK. Sherry is a certainty. Cocktails an adventure. (*He goes up* R. *to her.*)
LUCY. Cocktail!
BRISBY. Who else is expected, Miss French?
LUCY. Only one more. Mrs Corntonhart.

(MONK *takes the cocktail and returns to the easy chair* R.)

BRISBY. A peculiar name! (*He goes up to* CLAIRE, *with his back to the audience. To* CLAIRE.) I don't think we know the lady, do we?

(LUCY *sits on the arm of the settee and sips her sherry.*)

CLAIRE. No, I'm sure we don't.

(BRISBY *moves up to the settee* L.)

MONK. Corntonhart—(*Thinking.*) I've seen that name recently. Yes, of course! (*He moves a little down stage* R.)
CLAIRE. Tell us, Mr Monk.
MONK. Well, as a matter of fact....there was a rather formidable person having a row with a porter at the station. I noticed the name on her luggage.
CLAIRE. Corntonhart?
MONK. Yes.
BRISBY (*heavily*). A rather formidable person? Perhaps you will amplify that description?

(HENRIETTA *enters* R.)

MONK. I feel certain the lady will amplify it for herself. At the moment all I can suggest is something between Cleopatra and an angry mule.

CLAIRE. She sounds exciting.
HENRIETTA. Mrs Corntonhart.

(MRS CORTONHART *enters* R. *It is not altogether an inept description.* MRS CORNTONHART, *extremely well dressed is a good looking woman of about* ONDERSLEY'S *age. She has complete command of herself and generally of everybody else. Economical in speech, she delivers her remarks with a force that can be shattering. Her reaction is speedy as she is a firm believer in the value of getting her blow in first (and anywhere) though her aim is accurate to deadliness. Aware of the strength of her armament,* MRS CORNTONHART *is in no hurry to open the action. She surveys the room, and its contents, as though she were alone in it.* LUCY *comes hastily forward to deal with her.* HENRIETTA *exits* R.)

LUCY (*going up to the door*). I'm Lucy French, Mr Ondersley's secretary at the London branch. He is delayed on the phone.

(MRS CORNTONHART *takes her measure, and then turns away from* LUCY *without a word to the* R. *of the settee.*)

(*She is not taken aback.*) May I introduce Mrs Brisby .... Mrs Corntonhart.
CLAIRE. How do you do, Mrs Corn....Corn....? (*She hesitates.*)
MRS CORNTONHART (*immediately*). Corntonhart. One word, not two, Cornton, not corncrake, or cornflower. This your husband?
CLAIRE. Yes....
MRS CORNTONHART. How d'ye do?
BRISBY (*viewing her without enthusiasm*). How do you do?
LUCY. Dr Wadd. Mr Monk....Mrs Corntonhart.
WADD *and* MONK. How do you do?
MRS CORNTONHART. How d'ye do? How d'ye do? (*Suddenly turning on* LUCY.) Well, Miss I-forget-your-name, I suppose you're going to offer me a drink, aren't you?
LUCY (*moving up to the table above the settee*). Sherry, cocktail or gin and bitters?
MRS CORNTONHART.. Gin and bitters.
LUCY (*offering her a plate*). A biscuit, or perhaps you'd prefer candied peel?

(MRS CORNTONHART *looks at her, then turns away and pounces upon* MONK, *moving down stage to his* L.)

MRS CORNTONHART. You on the train?
MONK. Yes, I-er I....er, saw you, too. You were having some trouble with a porter....perhaps I should have....
MRS CORNTONHART. No, you shouldn't. Didn't need your help. Told him where to get off.
CLAIRE (*venturesomely*). That was his job to tell you, wasn't it?

(MRS CORNTONHART *gives a mirthless laugh, moving towards* BRISBY.)

MRS CORNTONHART (*to* BRISBY). I see your wife is a wit. (*She turns back to* MONK *again.*) Told him railway company paid him to move my luggage. Anything I chose to give him was out of charity.

(LUCY *comes down* R. *and hands* MRS CORNTONHART *her drink, and then sits on the pouffe down* C.)

BRISBY (*who would love to have the courage to do just the same thing; moving in a little*). In these so called democratic days, he would not like your telling him that.
MRS CORNTONHART. Dunno' in the least whether he liked it or not. But I will not be victimised.
MONK (*with an eyebrow raised*). I'm sure you won't. (*He sits in the easy chair* R.)
MRS CORNTONHART. Are you? Thank you. Porters think a woman travelling alone is a defenceless creature. I'm not.
MONK. I'm....
MRS CORNTONHART (*very quickly*). You're sure I'm not. Thank you again.
LUCY (*soothingly*). Mrs Corntonhart is right, of course. It's absurd when you come to think of it, all this tipping business.
MRS CORNTONHART (*accepting no olive branches*). That's surprising from you. Should have thought you'd take the employees' side.
LUCY. Because I'm Mr Ondersley's employee?
MONK (*hastily*). Weird job yours must be, Miss French. You get all sorts of people to deal with....
LUCY. Of course. Some very pleasant and (*after a slight pause*) others ....(*Very swiftly.*) Another gin and bitters, Mrs Corntonhart?
MRS CORNTONHART (*ignoring the insult*). Haven't finished this. Well, I suppose there's no harm sitting down, is there? (*She goes towards the settee.*)
CLAIRE (*making room for her on the settee*). Of course.

(BRISBY *moves down* L. *to the easy chair and sits.*)

(*Positions now are*—MRS CORNTONHART, *on the settee* R. CLAIRE *on the settee* L. BRISBY, *is in the armchair down* L. MONK, *in the armchair* R. DR WADD, *on the stool* L. LUCY *is on the pouffe.*)

MRS CORNTONHART (*to* WADD). You James Ondersley's doctor?
WADD. I am.
MRS CORNTONHART. Think he's mad?
WADD. Quite on the contrary.
BRISBY. I wonder what made you ask that question.
MRS CORNTONHART (*tartly*). Wanted to know the answer. Why does a hen cross the road?

MONK (*aside to* LUCY). Because its journey's really necessary.

BRISBY. Pardon my asking you, but Mr Ondersley did not by any chance....convey to you that he wanted you to be his guest this week-end as a matter of urgency?

MRS CORNTONHART (*staring at him*). As a matter of fact, he did. What's all this mean? Eh?....

BRISBY. It would be better to ask Mr Ondersley. I have no information upon the subject.

MRS CORNTONHART. So everyone's invited "urgently"?

CLAIRE. Yes.

BRISBY. It would appear so.

MRS CORNTONHART. Practical joke! People don't play practical jokes on me.

(ONDERSLEY *enters up* C. *smoking*.)

MONK. Not a second time, certainly!

MRS CORNTONHART. You seem to know me very well, young man. (*To* LUCY.) Where's Mr Ondersley?

ONDERSLEY. Here. (*He goes to the drink table*.) And delighted to see you all. How are you, Mrs Corntonhart? In good Corntonhart, I'm sure. Hello, Monk. Delighted you were able to come. Now, Miss French, have you introduced everybody?

LUCY. I think so.

ONDERSLEY (*coming down stage and crossing to the fireplace*). Fine. And are you all cocktailed, sherried, and ginned? And how go the inventions, Monk?

MONK. They do go. (*He hardly reciprocates* ONDERSLEY'S *cordiality*.)

ONDERSLEY. Splendid.

MRS CORNTONHART. Now, what about it?

ONDERSLEY. What about what?

MRS CORNTONHART. This urgent invitation business.

ONDERSLEY. Dear me, you all have such a low opinion of yourselves. Why shouldn't a man be urgently in need of (*he bows slightly to* CLAIRE) charming society? (*He sits on the* L. *arm of the settee*.)

CLAIRE. It's very nice of you to ask us, I think.

BRISBY. We....er....we all think, Ondersley, that it is high time you explained this peculiar wording of your invitations. A joke is a joke, but....

ONDERSLEY (*suddenly serious*). But my dear Brisby, who on earth suggested I was joking?

CLAIRE. You mean....?

ONDERSLEY. That when I said I urgently needed you all here, I meant just what I said. I urgently needed you. All of you.

DR WADD. You'd better explain, Ondersley.

MRS CORNTONHART. You had.

ONDERSLEY. A private matter .... very private .... I know you'll respect my confidence....

LUCY (*rising*). Would you like me to leave you?
ONDERSLEY (*to her*). I said I needed all of you, all, without exception.
BRISBY. In that case, let us have the explanation, without further delay.
ONDERSLEY (*rising and moving to the table above the settee*). All right ....but I didn't want to spoil your dinner.

(LUCY *resumes her seat.*)

CLAIRE. You sound perfectly gruesome, J.O.
ONDERSLEY (*pouring himself out a sherry as he speaks*). Gruesome? No, Claire. There wasn't anything gruesome....but there might have been. Well (*he drinks the sherry*) good luck, everyone .... You see, ladies and gentlemen....I have *one failing*, one failing you all know about. (*He crosses down to the candied peel table, taking up the box as he speaks.*) Candied peel....(*tapping the box with his finger*) candied peel!
BRISBY. What on earth has that got to do....?
ONDERSLEY (*silencing him with a gesture*). I can't resist the wretched stuff. You remember that, Mrs Corntonhart....you remember my weakness for candied peel? (*He puts down the box.*)
MRS CORNTONHART (*a trifle uncomfortably as it would seem*). Yes.... I do. (*She drinks.*)
ONDERSLEY. And you, Monk....you remember my chewing it in the office when you came to see me about that process of yours?
MONK (*after a slight hesitation*). Yes, I think so.
ONDERSLEY. With the rest of you it's common knowledge. (*He stubs out his cigarette.*) Well, I get the stuff sent to me every week by Tander and Maxims. Last week a new box arrived, it was left out on the settee ....and that little fox terrier of mine—Pinker—came in when there was no cne here and scoffed the lot, or nearly the lot.
CLAIRE. Well?
ONDERSLEY. Not so well for Pinker. I found him here—lying dead. He had been poisoned....(*He pauses.*)

(MRS CORNTONHART *drops her wine glass suddenly.*)

My dear Mrs Corntonhart....I've given you a shock. Careless of me. (*He swiftly picks up the glass.*) Let me give you another; gin and bitters, wasn't it? (*He smells the glass.*)
MRS CORNTONHART. Sorry....
ONDERSLEY (*pouring out a gin and bitters into the other glass*). My fault entirely.
DR. WADD (*putting his glass on the mantlepiece*). If you're serious, J.O., you've something more to tell us.
ONDERSLEY. Yes, I'm afraid I have. (*He returns the glass to* MRS CORNTONHART *and takes the decanter to* CLAIRE, *crossing towards the fireplace.*) Your glass is empty, Claire. (*He fills it up for her with sherry.*)

BRISBY. Are you really trying to persuade us the candied peel was poisoned ?

ONDERSLEY (*as he pours out* CLAIRE's *sherry*). What's that, Brisby ? (*Looking up.*) Yes; I'm afraid I am....Careful, Claire, my dear, you'll spill it. (*He returns to the table with the decanter.*)

MONK. You mean you had it analysed ?

ONDERSLEY (*picking up the gin*). Certainly.

BRISBY. This is not one of your—your funny stories, I presume, Ondersley ?

ONDERSLEY. I don't find it funny myself....Gin, Brisby ?

BRISBY. Thank you.

(ONDERSLEY *fills his glass and goes back to the table.*)

MONK. What was in the candied peel ?

ONDERSLEY (*walking across to him*). Some form of arsenic. Tetrasyll. As a chemist you'll know more about the stuff than I do. Cocktail ? (*He fills* MONK's *glass from the shaker and then returns to the table.*)

MRS CORNTONHART (*slowly*). What I don't understand is, what this has got to do with me.

ONDERSLEY. I'm coming to that. (*He takes a piece of candied peel from the box.*)

LUCY (*quickly*). Mr Ondersley....the candied peel !

ONDERSLEY. Oh, this is O.K. I bought it from the shop myself. Ready for a cocktail ? (*He puts back the shaker on the table.*)

LUCY. Not another, thanks.

ONDERSLEY. What has it got to do with all of you ? (*He crosses to the fireplace.*) Well, I can't really believe that the arsenic found its way into my candied peel of its own accord, and the reasonable conclusion is....someone must have put it there. Someone who knew I ate the stuff.

BRISBY. But that is fantastic.

ONDERSLEY. Entirely. It nearly made a fantasy of me.

CLAIRE (*who is perhaps more intent than any of the others*). Go on.

ONDERSLEY. I haven't much further to go. The obvious step seemed to be to make a little list of the people who knew my habits. There are others, of course, to be considered in due course—my Scottish office, for example, but....

MRS CORNTONHART (*angrily*). Suppose we must believe this extraordinary story, but I don't understand why you should have asked us here for the week-end. What has.... ?

ONDERSLEY. I've asked you....because I'm under the definite impression that one of *you* has attempted to poison me.

(HENRIETTA *comes in* R. *immediately at the end of his speech.*)

HENRIETTA. Dinner is ready, Sir.

ONDERSLEY (*easily*). And I'm sure we're all ready for dinner. Come along, won't you. (*He crosses to* MRS CORTONHART.) Mrs Cortonhart, may I ? (*He offers her his arm.*)

MRS CORTONHART *looks daggers at him as she takes it; and they are moving to the door as—*

the CURTAIN *falls*

SCENE 2.

SCENE—The same. After breakfast the next morning.

When the CURTAIN *rises* LUCY *is seated on the pouffe and is entering something in a note book, a newspaper is at her feet.* MONK *enters from* C. *He is smiling to himself.*

MONK. Well, the party seems to be going fine.
LUCY. Glad you like it.
MONK (*sitting on the settee*). It's unique. I've been at a lot of parties where the food made you think the host was trying to poison the guests....but for the guests to try to poison the host....it's terrific.
LUCY. Help yourself to cigarettes. You'll find some behind you.
MONK. Thanks. (*Taking the box, offering her one, and lighting both cigarettes.*) Tell me what happens in the second act ?
LUCY. The second act ?
MONK. Precisely. Act One,—Host announces that a guest has tried to murder him ; and for the rest of the evening refuses to discuss the matter at all....Obviously, the rest of the evening is the interval. Curtain goes up on second act, this morning—now.
LUCY. Where's all this leading us to ?
MONK. Think. Use your brains ! What's the first thing the detective would look for ?
LUCY. The detective ?
MONK (*with a gesture of despair*). The detective in the play, of course. What would he look for first ? Motive. Motive for the crime. I've got a little something some others haven't got.
LUCY. Does it hurt you much ?
MONK. If Mr Ondersley had passed out Mr Brisby would have succeeded him as Chairman of the Board, wouldn't he ?
LUCY. I suppose so.
MONK. And Brisby would have taken on my process which Ondersley wouldn't. There's a motive for you if you like ! With Ondersley

out of the way, behold fame and fortune for Oswald Monk. Damn it, it's enough to hang the Archbishop of Canterbury. (*He pauses for a second.*) If there wasn't enough already !

LUCY. It seems to amuse you. I don't think there's anything funny in anyone trying to poison Mr Ondersley.

MONK (*rises and moves to her ; with a sudden change in his voice*). Then why did *you* try to ?

LUCY (*rises and replaces the newspaper on the table above the easy chair*). I could poison one of his guests with pleasure.

MONK (*quickly following behind her to her* L.). Ah....that's an admission. You've got the poisoning habit. Poisoned candied peel.... the mark of a woman all over it....A woman. You....? Mrs Brisby....? Not Mrs Brisby....that's one thing certain.

LUCY (*turning*). Why so certain ? (*She walks to the fireplace and faces the mantelpiece.*)

MONK (*walking a little towards her in front of the settee*). If she'd poisoned anyone it would have been her husband years ago. But then there's Mrs Corntonhart. No, I can't associate poisoned candy with her. A blood-stained battle axe, perhaps. Then Brisby.... Perhaps he wanted to be the Chairman of the Ondersleys. I wonder if he sent the candied peel ?

LUCY (*facing him*). It's very wicked to talk like that behind Mr Brisby's back.

(BRISBY *enters the room* R. *He looks at* MONK *with an expression of dislike and seats himself in the easy chair* R.)

MONK (*to* LUCY). Well, here's Mr Brisby's front. Morning, sir. (*He sits on the settee.*)

BRISBY (*briefly*). Morning.

(LUCY *sits on the arm of the easy chair down* L.)

MONK (*easily*). I was just wondering whether you sent that poisoned stuff to J. Ondersley.

BRISBY (*rising and angrily turning on him*). If that is intended to be humorous, it is in the worst possible taste. (*He walks up to the table above the easy chair.*)

MONK. Don't be angry, please. Actually, I'm the favourite for the job.

BRISBY. You treat this grave matter as a complete joke ?

MONK. No, not complete....It won't be complete till our host tells us the answer.

BRISBY. Do you suggest that he knows it himself ?

MONK (*quietly*). Surely....or else there's no point in his method.

BRISBY (*picking up the newspaper, and looking at the headlines*). I don't follow you.

MONK. Well....Why put everybody on their guard by that extraordinary statement, and then point blank refuse to discuss it again.... unless....he's waiting for someone to confess.

BRISBY. I must refuse to take these speculations seriously. (*He moves down to the easy chair* R. *and sits with the paper.*)
MONK. Well, speculations or not, the detective will say....
BRISBY (*sharply*). What detective?
MONK (*patiently*). The hypothetical detective....
BRISBY. What *are* you talking about?
MONK. He'd say the first thing was to find a motive. I've suggested one for myself and one for you, but I can't plant one on Miss French ....yet.

(MRS SEDDONS *enters* R. *with the* "*Sunday Pictorial*" *and crosses to* LUCY.)

MRS SEDDONS. Good morning, Miss French. Here's your "Sunday Pictorial."
LUCY (*rising*). Thank you, Mrs Seddons. How's Henrietta's finger?
MRS SEDDONS. It's still looking nasty, Miss. Dr Wadd's coming to have a look at it.
MONK. I smell blood....What's happened?
MRS SEDDONS. Henrietta cut her finger on a broken glass last night, after dinner.
LUCY. Looking for clues? (*She sits in the easy chair with the newspaper.*)
MONK. Certainly. Like to make a bet I'll solve the mystery unaided? Heads I win....tails you....clues.
LUCY. You *are* an idiot.
BRISBY (*looking over his paper*). This sort of discussion is most ill-timed, most ill-timed, indeed.

(MRS SEDDONS *is about to depart, and crosses up to the door between the easy chair and the settee, as* MRS CORNTONHART, *followed by* CLAIRE, *now enters* R. *She is in fine fettle.*)

MRS SEDDONS (*to* MRS CORNTONHART). Good morning, madam.

(MONK *rises from the settee, walks to the fireplace, stubs out his cigarette in the ashtray on the mantelpiece and sits on the stool.*)

MRS CORNTONHART (*briefly*). Morning.
MRS SEDDONS. I hope you enjoyed your breakfast in bed, madam.
MRS CORNTONHART (*instantly; crossing in front of* MRS SEDDONS *to the settee*). Food in this house is extremely good....for a lunatic asylum.
MRS SEDDONS (*hardly believing her ears*). I beg your pardon....
MRS CORNTONHART. Shall be leaving on the evening train after dinner. You arrange for a car. (*She sits on the settee.*)
MRS SEDDONS. I'll try, madam, but it's Sunday....
MRS CORNTONHART. Thanks for the information. Day after Saturday generally is.

MONK (*rising and crossing over to the* R. *of* BRISBY). Seen the *Sunday Exposure*, Mr Brisby ? Fairly spread themselves on crime. Ought to give *us* a proper write-up.

BRISBY. I sincerely trust that no word of this....this lamentable episode will ever appear in the press.

CLAIRE (*to* MRS SEDDONS). What time is the post from here on Sundays, Mrs Seddons ?

MRS SEDDONS. Half-past three, ma'am.

(*She goes out* R., CLAIRE *crosses* L. *and sits on the* L. *of the settee.*)

MRS CORNTONHART (*pouncing on* LUCY). Want *you.*

LUCY. Is there something I can do for you ? (*Rising and moving to her.*)

MRS CORNTONHART. You said you were James Ondersley's secretary ?

LUCY. I am. At head office in London. Mr Blair is the secretary at the Edinburgh office.

MRS CORNTONHART. Where's Mr Ondersley ?

LUCY. He isn't up yet.

MRS CORNTONHART. Where's that ward of his ?

LUCY. Miss Lenner's away for the week-end.

MRS CORNTONHART. Sent her away whilst he ran this racket, eh ?

LUCY. I really have no idea what you're talking about.

MRS CORNTONHART. No. You're pretty dumb, aren't you. (*Her voice is rising in wrath.*)

LUCY. Perhaps....Mrs Corntonhart, but I'm not deaf. (*She sits on the stool.*)

MONK (*his hands in his pockets*). One up for the home team !

(MRS CORNTONHART *swings round on him, but he avoids her eye.*)

CLAIRE. Does....does Mr Ondersley intend to....talk about this ....this matter to-day, do you know, Lucy ?

LUCY. I'm afraid I'm as much in the dark as you are.

MRS CORNTONHART. Don't believe you.

LUCY. I don't think you were asked to.

MONK. Two up for the....(*Catching* MRS CORTONHART'S *eye.*) No score.

BRISBY. Let us endeavour to behave like reasonable people, not like children.

MONK. Hear, hear !

BRISBY (*viciously*). I was referring to you in particular.

MONK (*wilting*). Bit choppy in the straits to-day.

MRS CORNTONHART. Mr Brisby. You're Ondersley's partner.... What's he up to ?

MONK. It's all perfectly simple.

CLAIRE. Perfectly simple ?

MONK. Yes, you see....

BRISBY. I must refuse (*he rises*) to listen to any more of this nonsense.

Lucy. Don't mind him, Mrs Brisby, he's making a thriller out of the situation.

Monk (*to* Mrs Corntonhart). Just take a hypothetical case....

Brisby (*throws down the paper in the chair and crosses to the door up* c.). Perhaps, Miss French, you will tell me when Mr Ondersley comes down.

(Wadd *appears in the doorway* c.)

Dr Wadd. Good morning, everybody....(*Looking around him.*) I can almost guess what you're talking about.

Mrs Corntonhart. You can, can you. Dr Wadd ? Well, you ought to be able to tell us something.

Dr Wadd (*coming into the room, to the* l. *of the armchair* r.). Anything I can.

Mrs Corntonhart. This story of the poisoned candy .... is it all moonshine ?

Dr Wadd. Moonshine ?

Mrs Corntonhart. One of James Ondersley's practical jokes, or something ?

Brisby (*comes down a little*). A peculiar kind of practical joke, in my opinion.

Mrs Corntonhart. Weren't asked.

(Brisby *looks up in anger and moves to the table behind the settee.*)

Dr. Wadd. I can assure you it is not a practical joke.

Claire. You mean Mr Ondersley seriously believes one of us in this room actually sent him the candied peel.

Dr Wadd. Ah....that's rather a different question, isn't it ?

Mrs Corntonhart. Whether it is or not, what's your answer ?

Dr Wadd. I'm not prepared to give one.

Mrs Corntonhart. Why ?

Dr Wadd. Because each of us is able to answer that question for himself, isn't he....or (*slowly*)....isn't she ?

Brisby (*comes down to above* Wadd). Dr Wadd. Is it, or is it not a fact that Ondersley actually received poisoned candied peel ?

Dr Wadd (*after a slight pause*). It is.

Monk. With that arsenical in it ?

Dr Wadd. Yes.

Mrs Corntonhart. How d'ye know ?

Dr Wadd. Because (*he crosses to the door* r. *as he speaks*) I, personally, brought some of the stuff to the analysts and saw their report. If you'll excuse me,...there's a maid I want to see.

Lucy (*about to rise*). I'll bring her to you.

Dr Wadd. Don't worry, thanks, I know where I'll find Mrs Seddons.

Claire (*rising and crossing to* Wadd). Just one more question, Dr Wadd....please.

DR WADD. Yes.
CLAIRE. That poison....the....the arsenic. It could have got in accidentally? Couldn't it.
DR WADD. I'm afraid not, Mrs Brisby. Both the analysts and the manufacturers are quite certain the poison was deliberately sweetened and added to the sugar covering the peel....And now....If you'll excuse me.

(*He goes out* R. *There is a silence for an appreciable moment after he has gone.*)

MONK (*moving to the fireplace and getting a cigarette from the mantelpiece*). So it's a pukka attempted murder. (*Moving to the easy chair* R. *and sitting.*) As Shakespeare would say....bloodier and bloodier!
BRISBY. But who....who in God's name, I ask you, would wish to poison Ondersley. The whole thing sounds wildly impossible. (*He moves to the easy chair down* L.)
CLAIRE (*crossing to the stool and sitting next to* LUCY). But Leonard.... I told you....I told you....
MRS CORNTONHART (*who has been watching* CLAIRE *keenly*). *What* did your wife tell you, Mr Brisby?
BRISBY (*facing her angrily*). I'd be glad if you'd mind your own business. My wife took this matter as serious from the start. I did not. Apparently I was wrong, but (*virtuously*) I acted according to my lights.
MRS CORNTONHART. According to your lights! Your batteries need recharging.
BRISBY. *Really*, Madam!
MRS CORNTONHART. I'd like to know why Mrs Brisby was so certain.
BRISBY. Are you trying to suggest....? (*He sits in the easy chair.*)
LUCY. There's nothing remarkable in Mrs Brisby's being certain Mr Ondersley wasn't joking. I never thought he was, either.
MRS CORNTONHART. My remarks weren't addressed to you.
LUCY. For that matter, I was speaking to Mr Brisby.
MONK (*about to make a remark, checks himself, and looks at them both*). The Umpire has gone home for his tea!
MRS. CORNTONHART. If you think I intend to wait till James Ondersley chooses to cease being mysterious, you're greatly mistaken.
BRISBY. I have known my partner for nearly twenty years. He can be irritating....extremely irritating at times; but he is not the sort of man who would have enemies.
MONK. I don't think that matters. For really dirty work, give me a friend every time.
BRISBY (*angrily*). That remark shows remarkably little sense.
MONK. It shows a remarkable amount of experience.

(MRS SEDDONS *enters* R. *followed by* ARTHUR HARRIS. *He is twenty-five or six, and is well tailored and quite at ease. There is nothing very distinctive about his appearance. He wears glasses, and has a quick, rather incisive, way of speaking.*)

MRS SEDDONS. Miss French, Mr Harris to see Mr Ondersley.

LUCY (*rising and crossing to him; in some surprise*). Good morning. Mr Harris, I am....

HARRIS (*shaking hands*). Mr Ondersley's secretary. How do you do?

LUCY. How do you do....Mr Ondersley was expecting you?

HARRIS. Oh yes.

LUCY. I'm very sorry, but I'm afraid he's not down yet.

HARRIS. No?

LUCY. I hardly think he will be down much before lunch.

HARRIS. Then I'm afraid Mohammed must go to the mountain.... Perhaps you'll show me the way?

LUCY (*after a slight hesitation*). Mrs Seddons, perhaps you would tell Mr Ondersley....

HARRIS (*quietly*). I don't really think you need worry. Mr Ondersley is expecting me at this hour and wanted to see me immediately I arrived. So (*to* MRS SEDDONS) if you'll show me where his room is....

(MRS SEDDONS *looks at* LUCY, *who nods.*)

LUCY. Will you take Mr Harris to Mr Ondersley's room?

MRS SEDDONS. This way, sir. (*She goes towards the door up* C. *followed by* MR HARRIS.)

HARRIS (*opening the door up* C.). After you.

MRS SEDDONS. Thank you, sir.

(*She goes out up* C. HARRIS *is about to go.*)

MONK (*rising and going to* L. *of* HARRIS; *excitedly*). Just a second, Mr Harris. Excuse my butting in, but....I have a theory....You're not by any chance an hypothetical detective, are you?

HARRIS (*laughing*). Good Lord! no.

MONK. Sorry....my mistake.

HARRIS. There's nothing hypothetical about me. I'm an inspector from Scotland Yard.

(*He goes out up* C.)

MONK. Good Heavens! (*He is completely flabbergasted by the reply and staggers across to the easy chair* R. *and sits.*) Of course, I knew he was all the time!

(LUCY *moves to the pouffe.*)

BRISBY (*rising*). But this is monstrous....absolutely monstrous.

CLAIRE (*rising*). He's actually called in the police!

MRS CORNTONHART. A put-up job! (*To* LUCY.) You knew this man was coming.

LUCY. Indeed, I did not.

MONK. Of course she didn't. *I* knew....(*he looks round at the others and adds, weakly*) hypothetically.
CLAIRE. What does it mean ?
MONK. Act two, with a vengeance.

(*The telephone rings.* LUCY *rises and crosses to the table and picks up the receiver.*)

LUCY. Hello....Yes....This is Arrowley 68....Thank you.... Hello....Yes....(*With surprise in her voice.*) That you, Grace ? ....I'm sorry....how grim....Yes, of course. You'll be back this afternoon. Right. I'm awfully sorry....Good-bye. (*She puts down the receiver. To* CLAIRE, *coming down* L. *and sitting on the stool.*) Harry Williamson. You know....the people Grace is staying with ....he's got appendicitis. They operated early this morning. Grace is coming back this afternoon.
BRISBY. A nice situation she is to return to.
MRS CORNTONHART. Why did he send her away ?
CLAIRE (*to* LUCY). Do you think Grace knew anything about....about all this ?
LUCY. I'm sure she didn't.
MRS CORNTONHART (*rising, and crossing to* R. *a little*). I'm going to leave this madhouse immediately.
MONK. People in madhouses aren't let out of them. You ought to know that.
MRS CORNTONHART (*furiously turning on him*). That is an impertinence, young man. (*To* LUCY.) Will you kindly get a car for me ? There's a train at one-thirty, I believe.
LUCY. I'm afraid there isn't. Not on Sundays. There's only the evening train at nine-fifteen.
MRS CORNTONHART. Then I'll get a car from London. (*She moves to the telephone.*)
CLAIRE. Wouldn't it....wouldn't it be better to wait and see....?
MRS CORNTONHART. Thank you. Advice not needed.
BRISBY. I think my wife is right. It is no answer to this accusation to run away.
MRS CORNTONHART. Run away !....Like to see the situation I'd run away from.
MONK (*with profound conviction*). I wouldn't.
BRISBY. Just a moment, please. (*He moves up to the fireplace.*) This is an unthinkable situation. We are—or one of us—is accused of attempted murder. The arrival of this Inspector from Scotland Yard is the final proof—incredible as it may seem—that my partner is in earnest.
MRS CORNTONHART. Is he ?

(HARRIS *enters up* C. *He speaks directly to* LUCY.)

HARRIS. The telephone? (*To* MRS CORNTONHART.) I'm sorry I shall have to phone immediately. (*He moves up to the telephone.*)

(MRS CORNTONHART *moves down to the* L. *end of the settee.*)

BRISBY (*pompously*). I shall go up now, and speak to Ondersley.
HARRIS (*looking up*). No....I'm afraid you can't do that.
BRISBY. Indeed? And why not, may I enquire?
HARRIS. Mr Ondersley is dead.
MRS CORNTONHART. Dead....dead!
HARRIS (*into phone*). Hello, will you get me Lambeth 229, please? Yes, Lambeth 229.

QUICK CURTAIN

ACT II.

SCENE 1.

SCENE—the same. Before dinner the same day.

When the CURTAIN *rises* LUCY *is sitting on the* R. *arm of the settee talking to* HARRIS, *who is on the stool in front of the fireplace.*

HARRIS. Of course, the cause of Mr Ondersley's death cannot be finally determined until expert examination has been made. The strong presumption is....that he was poisoned.

LUCY. Couldn't it have been his heart ?

HARRIS. Yes. Dr Wadd is careful not to express an opinion. But Mr Ondersley was in perfect health. And we *do* know an attempt to poison him was made a few weeks ago.

LUCY. By one of the persons he invited for the week-end. When did he ask you ?

HARRIS. He called on me a few days ago—told me an attempt had been made to poison him—and promised me the complete story when I saw him this morning. Tell me, Miss French, how long have you been Mr Ondersley's secretary ?

LUCY. Between eight and nine years.

HARRIS (*rising and crossing to* R.C.) Was it a usual thing for him to ask you here ?

LUCY. No—not personally, I mean—I've been here a good many times as Miss Lenner's guest for tennis parties and that sort of thing.

HARRIS. So his asking you to come was quite unexpected. Did he give any particular reason for the invitation ?

LUCY. Yes, he said Miss Lenner would be away, and asked me to act as hostess for his guests.

HARRIS. Rather an unusual request ? (*He moves up stage towards the table above the easy chair.*)

LUCY. Yes....I....

HARRIS. It seems that he went to particular trouble to have you here on this particular occasion.

LUCY. Apparently.

HARRIS. That—pardon my saying it—is another way of saying he was particular to include you in his list of suspected persons.

LUCY. I suppose it was.

HARRIS. Do you know any of the staff at the Scottish Office—Mr Blair, the Secretary, for example ?

LUCY. No. The two offices are practically separate organisations.

HARRIS. And this habit of Mr Ondersley's, of eating candied peel. He kept some at the office ?

LUCY. Oh yes.

HARRIS. Did he eat this stuff when he was interviewing callers ?

LUCY. He used to keep the candied peel in a drawer and take an occasional piece if he was talking to someone he knew well, like Mr Brisby.

HARRIS. Or yourself, of course.

LUCY. Of course.

HARRIS (*crossing back to the stool*). So, it's safe to say that this little habit of his was only known to quite a few people at his office. (*He sits on the stool.*)

LUCY. Very few.

HARRIS. Which explains why he asked a few chosen people down for this week-end. What about the lady with the extraordinary name, Mrs Corntonhart ? She is apparently one of the few who knew about the candied peel habit. Can you explain that ?

LUCY I never heard of her before.

(MONK *enters up* C. *and looks at them in some amusement.*)

MONK (*agreeably*). If I'm intruding you have only got to say the word ....and nothing will persuade me to leave you. (*He moves down* R. *of the easy chair.*)

HARRIS (*briefly*). Thanks.

MONK. So glad. I wouldn't like to be in the way. You see, Inspector, I have an hypothesis.

HARRIS. Another. *I* was one, wasn't I ?

MONK (*unperturbed*). Yes. I imagined you....therefore you *were*.

LUCY. For goodness sake don't waste Mr Harris' time. Why not take a walk to the local hypothesis.

MONK. It isn't open yet. Well....I'll leave you in peace. But I warn you, Inspector, that we amateurs....

HARRIS. Amateurs ?

MONK. Amateur detectives, we all have our methods....(*He takes a large magnifying glass from his pocket.*) I borrowed this magnifying glass from the library, Miss French ; I hope you don't mind ?

LUCY. What on earth's the idea ?

MONK. An aid to scientific detection. It shows you things that aren't there....most useful for a detective.

LUCY (*annoyed*). Do stop fooling. You seem to forget....

MONK (*looking at the magnifying glass*). Can also be used for harnessing the rays of the sun to boil eggs—when there's any sun....and.... of course....when there are any eggs. Well, I'll leave you to your own investigation. (*He takes a few steps towards the door up* C. *Suddenly serious.*) By the way, Inspector, I *can* make one suggestion....

HARRIS. I'd be very glad to have it.

MONK. It might make things a little easier for you.

HARRIS. Thank you.

MONK (*with a suggestion of mystery*). Well....look....look carefully ....on the bookshelf in Mrs Corntonhart's bedroom beside her bed.
HARRIS. What shall I find there?
MONK. Dirty books!

(*He exits up* C.)

HARRIS. Is he always like that?
LUCY. More or less.
HARRIS. Doesn't take life—or death—too seriously, does he?
LUCY. He ought to be ashamed of himself.
HARRIS. Well. Let's get back to it....Did you attend to all Mr Ondersley's correspondence, the private as well as the business?
LUCY. Yes, but there were other letters that came to him at the office which he never told me about.
HARRIS. Mrs Corntonhart might have been one of those correspondents?
LUCY. Certainly. But I don't know.
HARRIS. Quite. Tell me about Mr Ondersley's relations with Mr Brisby. How is it that the younger man—Mr Ondersley—was the Chairman of the Board?
LUCY. Mr Ondersley's father founded the firm and handed on the chairmanship to his son.
HARRIS. Over the head of Mr Brisby?
LUCY. Yes, if you put it that way.
HARRIS. Did Mr Brisby accept the situation, or was he resentful about it?
LUCY (*rising and crossing to the easy chair* R., *hesitating*). I don't think I really ought to answer questions about Mr Ondersley's partner.
HARRIS. (*rising*). Mr Brisby did resent the position?
LUCY. Yes. I think he did.
HARRIS. And does still?
LUCY. I suppose so....Yes....I think....perhaps he does.
HARRIS (*going to her* L.). I heard, purely by accident, that Mrs Brisby and Mr Ondersley were....quite close friends....before she got married.
LUCY (*sitting on the arm of the easy chair* R.). I don't think there's any secret about that.
HARRIS. Mr Monk—he submitted an invention to Mr Ondersley, didn't he?
LUCY. Yes. Mr Brisby was very keen on it, and so were the experts, but Mr Ondersley turned it down.
HARRIS. And so it wasn't taken up. It seems a pity if it was a good invention.....but probably there wasn't much in it.
LUCY (*rising; quickly*). There was a great deal; it was a brilliant idea.
HARRIS (*smiling*). Mr Monk has one advocate, at least. Now that Mr Ondersley is dead I suppose Mr Brisby will succeed him as Chairman of the Board, and Mr Monk's process will be taken on by the firm.
LUCY. Mr Brisby will certainly be the new Chairman. Of course, what they'll do about Mr Monk's invention, I don't know. (*She sits in the easy chair.*)

HARRIS (*laughing*). But you've got a pretty good idea. (*He moves to the front of the settee.*) Tell me about Monk, he seems a rather brilliant person. You've known him a long time?
LUCY (*a shade cautiously, perhaps*). Yes....
HARRIS. And you've known him very well?
LUCY. We've been good friends.
HARRIS. Quite....What about Dr Wadd?
LUCY. Dr Wadd. Why....he's the doctor in Arrowsley.
HARRIS. Mr Ondersley's doctor?
LUCY. Yes....But more his friend, perhaps.

(MRS SEDDONS *comes in* R. *as they are speaking.*)

They used to play chess together.
HARRIS. Oh, Mrs Seddons, I wanted you. Have you a moment to spare?
MRS SEDDONS. Of course, sir.
LUCY. You don't want me any more? (*She rises.*)
HARRIS. Not for the present, thanks.

(LUCY *moves towards the door* C.)

MRS SEDDONS. Dinner will be ready at half-past seven, Miss French.
LUCY. Thanks.

(LUCY *goes out up* C.)

HARRIS. Sit down, please, Mrs Seddons. You've been with Mr Ondersley a long time? (HARRIS *moves towards the fireplace. He gets a cigarette from the mantelpiece and lights it.*)
MRS SEDDONS. Oh, yes sir. Since he came to Arrowsley, nine years ago. (*She sits in the easy chair* R.)
HARRIS (*standing in front of the stool*). He was always a healthy man, wasn't he?
MRS SEDDONS. Indeed, he was, sir. Apart from an occasional few days with influenza or something like that I've never known him to be ill.
HARRIS. That's a tribute to the care you took of him.
MRS SEDDONS. I did my best. I can't understand his....his dying like this. No one was more full of life.
HARRIS. Never had any heart trouble you knew of?
MRS SEDDONS. Never!
HARRIS. And he was a very....moderate man?
MRS SEDDONS. Oh, very, though he used always to say "After luncheon walk a mile, after dinner drink awhile...." I don't think I've got that quite right, sir.
HARRIS. This trick of eating candied peel—that never seemed to upset him?

MRS SEDDONS. It never did, sir, though I often told him his stomach with all that peel inside, must be like a boiling of marmalade !
HARRIS. He used to eat so very much, did he ?
MRS SEDDONS. He was addicted to it....On and off, so to speak. There might be a week when he wouldn't touch it, and then he'd be eating it all the time, just as you might smoke a cigarette.
HARRIS. A funny habit.
MRS SEDDONS. Bachelors over forty get funny habits, sir. The poor creatures !
HARRIS. How used he to get the stuff ? Did he bring it from town with him ?
MRS SEDDONS. Oh, no, sir. It used to come by post from Tander and Maxims.
HARRIS. Several boxes, or one at a time ?
MRS SEDDONS. Sometimes one and sometimes several. Just what Mr Ondersley happened to have ordered, I suppose.
HARRIS. Thanks, Mrs Seddons.

(*She rises.*)

There's one thing more ; will you try and find Mrs Brisby and send her to me ?
MRS SEDDONS. She's in the sun parlour by herself. I'll ask her to come to you.
HARRIS. Thank you, Mrs Seddons.

(MRS SEDDONS *goes out* R. HARRIS, *when she has gone, stubs out his cigarette and walks to the candied peel table. He takes a box of candied peel from it and opens it, smelling it curiously. He puts it down, and looks round the room, then sees a letter on the mantelpiece. As he has it in his hands he hears someone tapping on the door* R. *He replaces the letter on the mantelpiece.*)

HARRIS (*turning round*). Who's that ?

(MISS PETHINGTON *appears in the doorway* R. *She is not in her very clearest mood.*)

HARRIS. Come in, won't you ?
MISS PETHINGTON. But....I'm afraid I'm intruding....? (*She looks at him questioningly.*)
HARRIS (*a little puzzled*). I am sure you're not.
MISS PETHINGTON. If you're quite sure....certain....sure....
HARRIS. You wanted to see Mr Ondersley....?
MISS PETHINGTON (*with sudden vigour*). But no, no, no. That is why I popped in through the french window in the dining room. Why should you think *that* ?

HARRIS (*smiling*). Well....Why shouldn't I....?

MISS PETHINGTON (*moving to the* R. *of the easy chair* R.). But you see. (*Dropping her voice in a whisper.*) ....You see, I should be at church. (*She gives almost a guilty start as she says it.*)

HARRIS (*with a slight gesture of despair*). Should you?

MISS PETHINGTON. But, of course....I'm the choir, you know.

HARRIS. All of it?

MISS PETHINGTON (*apologetically*). Well .... yes .... you see, it's a very *small* church....But ....Mr Ondersley doesn't go....to church.

HARRIS. Doesn't he?

MISS PETHINGTON. No....no....But he's very interested in it.

HARRIS. In church?

MISS PETHINGTON. No. No .... in Eugenics. Yes. The science by which....Dear me!....I've forgotten what science it is....

HARRIS. So Mr Ondersley was interested in Eugenics?

MISS PETHINGTON (*ecstatically*). Interested. He was *absorbed* in it. And he was giving me a cheque.

HARRIS (*delicately*). For your....your Eugenics?

MISS PETHINGTON. Well .... not *mine personally*....not personally ....Of course, that's what I came for—Mr Ondersley's cheque! He said he would leave it for me.

HARRIS. Perhaps he did. There's a letter here. May I ask what your name is?

MISS PETHINGTON (*taken aback*). My name....*my* name....of course ....(*She looks a little blank.*)

HARRIS. Yes. (*Gently.*) You do remember that, don't you?

MISS PETHINGTON (*helplessly*). The Vicar calls me Pussy....

HARRIS. Oh....?

MISS PETHINGTON. Only when we're alone, of course....*Only when we're alone.* (*She wanders up to the table behind the settee.*)

HARRIS. That's very thoughtful of him, I'm sure.

MISS PETHINGTON. Yes, he is a dear little man .... a dear little man. (*Suddenly.*) *Pethington*!

HARRIS. The Vicar's name is Pethington?

MISS PETHINGTON. But how naughty, *naughty* you are. That's *my* name!

HARRIS. Perhaps it won't be long if the Vicar calls you Pussy. But Miss Pethington, I think I've got what you want. Here we are (*taking a letter from the mantelpiece*) Miss Pethington.

MISS PETHINGTON (*coming round to the front of the settee and taking the letter*). Oh thank you, thank you....How good, good of him! (*She moves towards the table above the easy chair* R.)

HARRIS. And is that all you require?

MISS PETHINGTON (*now looking at the box of candied peel on the table*). You know he....he offered *me* some of that....(*she moves above the table, towards the door* R.).

HARRIS. That was nice of him.

MISS PETHINGTON (*pausing and turning to him*). Yes. And I refused....

Do you know why....?

HARRIS. No.

MISS PETHINGTON (*confidentially and with a hand over her middle*). Because it upsets my stom....(*She checks herself.*) It gives me windy ....(*She pauses again aghast.*) I mean....indi....yes *indi*gestion.

HARRIS. I'm sorry !

MISS PETHINGTON (*suddenly*). Look at the time....the time.... the time !

HARRIS (*glancing at the clock on the mantelpiece*). What time ?

MISS PETHINGTON. Time, time !....Sixty seconds make a minute, sixty minutes make an hour, twelve hours, one rod, pole or perch.

HARRIS. Really !

MISS PETHINGTON. What *am* I saying ? Good morning....good morning. Of....of course....it's the afternoon, isn't it ? Well ....good night !

(*She rushes off* R. *leaving* HARRIS *gazing at her in astonishment.* HARRIS *with a gesture of despair, takes another cigarette, lights it, and throws himself into the easy chair down* L. *As he does so,* CLAIRE *comes in up* C.)

CLAIRE (*who is pale and nervous in manner*). You wanted to see me, Mr Harris ? (*She walks down stage to the* R. *of the easy chair.*)

HARRIS. Yes. (*He passes his hand over his forehead, recovers himself and rises and goes to her.*) Thank you for coming. I only wanted to ask you a few questions....

CLAIRE (*quickly*). I'm afraid there's....there's nothing I can tell you, Mr Harris, but....

HARRIS. There may not be anything that you think useful, but there may be something that doesn't seem of much importance to you, and yet might help. Won't you sit down ? (*He leads her to the settee.*)

CLAIRE. But, really....I....

HARRIS. Yes, I know. (*He crosses to the fireplace.*) You must be deeply distressed....you and Mr Ondersley were such old friends. (*She sits on the settee.*)

CLAIRE. We were, indeed.

HARRIS. That was even before you met your husband ?

CLAIRE. Yes.

(HARRIS *takes out his case and offers her a cigarette.*)

Thank you.

(*He lights her cigarette, and returns to the stool and sits.*)

HARRIS. Don't be surprised at what I am now asking you. And please don't misunderstand it. Your husband's relations with Mr Ondersley —they were always very friendly ?

CLAIRE. Yes.

HARRIS. Always ?

CLAIRE. Yes. They had the usual disagreements over business matters of course....

HARRIS. Yes....of course, but....I wonder how I should put it ....Would you have said that your husband was jealous of Mr Ondersley ?

CLAIRE (*hesitating*). No....no I wouldn't.

HARRIS (*slowly*). For any reason ?

CLAIRE (*quietly*). For no reason.

HARRIS. Thank you, Mrs Brisby. May I ask you one more—I am afraid, rather leading—question ? Have you any idea in your mind as to who sent the poisoned candied peel to Mr Ondersley ?

CLAIRE (*after a second's hesitation*). You have no right to ask me that question.

HARRIS. No.... I don't think I have. But, I would like you to answer it all the same.

CLAIRE. Of course I have no idea....No idea whatever....

HARRIS. No....? You knew of course about Mr Ondersley's habit of eating the stuff ?

CLAIRE. Yes, of course I did. Anyone who knows J.O.....Mr Ondersley....well, would know that.

HARRIS. And you and your husbsnd would know him as well as anyone ?

CLAIRE. Certainly we would. My husband and he were partners.

HARRIS. One last question and, again, please don't misunderstand me. You never sent Mr Ondersley any candied peel yourself, did you ? At any time ? It would be a natural enough gesture....

CLAIRE. No....I did not....never.

HARRIS. Thank you. I hope I don't seem to have asked you a lot of unkind questions but, you see we can only get at the truth by asking everybody. (*He smiles.*) No matter how unlikely they may seem.

CLAIRE. Yes....of course I understand....Mr Harris....May I ask you one question in return ?

HARRIS. Certainly.

(WADD *enters up* C. *as* CLAIRE *asks her question.*)

CLAIRE. Is it established that Mr Ondersley was poisoned....? Certain, I mean....not just suspected ?

HARRIS. That's a question I can't answer. Perhaps Dr Wadd would give you more information than I can.

DR WADD (*coming down to the* L. *of the easy chair* R.). Good afternoon, Mrs Brisby. How can I help ?

CLAIRE (*rising and moving to* DR WADD). Dr Wadd, is it certain that....

DR WADD. I know what you're going to ask me. Much as I'd like to, I just can't tell you. We shall know the answer to-night. Till then you must be patient, my dear.

(CLAIRE *returns to the settee and sits.*)

HARRIS (*rising and moving towards the door up* C.). I must have another shot at getting a call through to London on the phone. Does the phone ever work in these parts of the world, Doctor ?

DR WADD. I assure you, in my house it never stops working.

(HARRIS *laughs and goes out up* C. DR WADD *sits on the settee with* CLAIRE.)

DR WADD. You're terribly worried, I'm afraid.

CLAIRE. It's such a horrible....horrible position to be in.

DR WADD. Of course it is....Just as much for me as for everyone else, you must remember....I was invited, exactly as the rest of you were.

CLAIRE. But what is going to happen ? How are they going to find out ? And if they do....(*She buries her face in her hands.*)

DR WADD. My dear, I think you are troubling yourself without reason. J.O. loved being unusual, and doing all sorts of bizarre things, but there was a very keen intellect behind the things he did. He wouldn't have planned anything that would make you suffer.

CLAIRE (*rising and crossing to below the fireplace*). No, he wouldn't.... I know that....he was too good a pal for that....But don't you see, it's all different now. This man Harris, and the police....J.O. hadn't planned all that.

DR WADD. I'm sure he had. Indeed, we know he had.

CLAIRE. But not without his being there, too.... to control things. Now it's all out of his hand....and anything can happen. Scandal ....publicity...

DR WADD (*moving to her and putting his hands on her shoulder*). It's hard to ask you to believe it, I know, but I do want you to feel that perhaps all this is working out, in J.O.'s absence, just as he planned it....

(GRACE LENNER *now comes in up* C. *She comes to* CLAIRE *and kisses her.* WADD *is clearly disconcerted at her appearance.*)

GRACE. Claire....darling.

(WADD *moves up to the* R. *of the settee.*)

CLAIRE. Grace....I'm ashamed of....going on like this when it's you who have really suffered the loss.

GRACE (*slowly*). It's all our loss. (*She moves up to the settee.*) Good afternoon, Dr. Wadd.

DR WADD (*abruptly*). Good afternoon. Excuse my rudeness, Grace but why on earth have you come back ? I didn't intend to tell you till to-night, when we knew a little more.

GRACE. Harry Williamson was taken ill. Appendicitis....They had to operate early this morning. I phoned Lucy, didn't she tell you ?

DR WADD (*level with her ; slowly*). No....I wish she had. I wonder, would you take my advice now ?

GRACE. Your advice. Yes. I'm sure I would.

DR WADD (*earnestly*). Go away again .... Anywhere .... The Lamberts would put you up....or we could, my housekeeper would be delighted....

GRACE. But I couldn't....I couldn't now. Why would you want me to....?

DR WADD. Only until to-morrow. Till we know something more about the truth of things....It will spare you any amount of anxiety, and being asked questions by Mr Harris. Don't you agree, Mrs Brisby ?

CLAIRE (*after a slight hesitation*). Yes....Yes, I'm sure you're right, Doctor.

GRACE. But I couldn't think of such a thing....even for a second.... why I must be here, I of all people....

CLAIRE (*moving up to* GRACE). Dr Wadd's right, Grace. There's no object in putting yourself through suffering that can be avoided.

DR WADD. Exactly. Look here, Mrs Brisby, just let Grace and me have a little pow-wow together. If I put on my very best bedside manner....

GRACE. No....I....

CLAIRE. My nose will do with a little powdering, anyhow.

(CLAIRE *goes out up* R.)

GRACE (*to* WADD). I don't understand why....

DR WADD (*into whose voice has come a note of urgency*). Who told you all about this ? Lucy French ?

GRACE. Yes. I met her as I was coming in.

DR WADD. And she told you everything ?

GRACE. About J.O..... ? Yes.

DR WADD. And what happened before dinner last night ?

GRACE. Yes. What does it all mean....?

DR. WADD. Whatever it means I am sure J.O. would not have wished you here now. You know a man has come from Scotland Yard ?

GRACE. Yes.

DR WADD (*sharply*). Have....has he seen you yet ?

GRACE. No, I came straight in here after leaving Lucy.

DR WADD. Then there's no need for him to know you've been home at all. I should just go away again, my dear, until the morning....or till I ring you.

GRACE. But that'd be impossible....it would seem like running away.

DR WADD. What have you to run away from ?

GRACE. That's just it....what have I ? (*She sits on the settee.*)

DR WADD. I suppose I've used the wrong argument.

GRACE. I'm afraid you have.

DR WADD (*seriously*). But, all the same, I urge you to do what I advise you.
GRACE. It's most sweet and thoughtful of you....But I couldn't.... J.O. would understand....I know he'd understand.
DR WADD (*slowly, after a pause, and crossing* L. *to the fireplace*). He was very fond of you, Grace.
GRACE. I was very fond of him.
DR WADD. How fond ?
GRACE. As much as....(*She makes a gesture.*) As much as I could be.
DR WADD. And he of you....Why didn't you....? He thought there was someone else. You knew he thought that ?
GRACE (*slowly*). Yes, I did. At first....but there wasn't....no one else.
DR WADD (*going to the settee and sitting beside* GRACE). He'd be happy to know that now....wouldn't he ? Why not do what he wished—what he planned ? Why not let him still play his game....his own way ?
GRACE. That was when he was alive. But now that he's dead, he can't try to spare me anything....
DR WADD. Nor you him. What's the use of going through all this when you need not ?
GRACE. All the others have to go through with it, haven't they ?
DR WADD. Yes....but aren't you forgetting that one of them—he believed—had tried to poison him ?
GRACE. And aren't you forgetting that all of them—not merely the guilty one—are going through it now. I'm not going to have to suffer more than anyone else who isn't guilty. (*She rises and goes to the mantel-piece, for a cigarette.*)
DR WADD (*slowly*). I wonder. Look here, Grace, we're old friends, aren't we ? Will you let me....

(*As he speaks* HARRIS *enters the room up* C., WADD *breaks off abruptly, with a shrug of his shoulders and rises.*)

This is Mr Harris, from Scotland Yard....Miss Lenner.

(HARRIS *pauses for a moment.*)

HARRIS (*without coming forward*). How do you do....Miss Lenner ?
GRACE (*lighting the cigarette and without looking up*). How do you do ?
HARRIS. That telephone....
DR WADD. You haven't had any luck yet ?
HARRIS. No, I can't get any answer at all.
GRACE. Mr Harris. (*She goes over to* HARRIS.) If there's anything I can tell you.... (*She breaks off abruptly.*)

(*They stand looking at each other for a moment in silence as* HENRIETTA *enters* R.)

HARRIS (*turning away from her*). Not for the moment, I think, thank you, Miss Lenner. I'll let you know, of course....

HENRIETTA (*whose hand is bandaged*). The telephone, sir. There's a call coming through to you....from London, I think. In the library.

HARRIS. Thank you. (*To the others.*) You'll excuse me.

(*He goes out up* C. GRACE *looks after him as he goes.*)

DR WADD (*quickly*). Hello, Henrietta. How's the finger ?

HENRIETTA. It's better, thanks, Doctor. Throbs a bit still.

DR WADD. I should think it does. Didn't I tell you to keep your arm in a sling ?

HENRIETTA (*moving towards* DR WADD). I didn't think it would matter, I'm not using it really.

DR WADD. She cut it smashing your glasses.

GRACE (*coming down to the* L. *of* HENRIETTA). I'm sorry, Henrietta.

DR WADD. Let's have a look at it. (*Sharply.*) Come on, Grace, do your stuff, get that bandage off for me.

(HENRIETTA *sits on the arm of the settee.* GRACE *hesitates, then takes* HENRIETTA'S *hand in hers and begins to undo the bandage.* MONK *enters up* C.)

DR WADD. Not that I mind taking off a bandage, it's putting them on I object to. The damn things never stay on.

GRACE. This is off now. Am I hurting you ?

HENRIETTA. Not a bit, Miss Grace.

DR WADD. If I did that she'd scream the house down.

MONK (*looking over their shoulders with the keenest interest*). Do you think we'll be able to save the arm, Doctor ?

GRACE. Hello, Oswald.

MONK. Hello, hello. Immediate amputation, I'd suggest. I'll give the anaesthetic.

HENRIETTA. Oh, sir !

MONK. Nothing to be frightened of in an anaesthetic. Had one myself last spring. Tip-top doctor gave me the stuff. Came round alive and kicking.

DR WADD (*meaningly*). Don't blame him, Mr Monk. Even tip-top doctors make mistakes sometimes.

MONK. Look here....

DR WADD. There we are. (*He looks at the finger.*) Yes.. .it's getting on nicely. It'd be a good idea if you were to give it a soaking in saline—just as I told you this morning....and then ? Grace, will you bandage it up again ?

HENRIETTA (*rising and going to the door* R.). Thank you, Doctor.

GRACE. I'll be along in a few minutes with the bandage.

(MONK *goes down left as* HENRIETTA *opens the door.* BRISBY *enters* R. WADD *goes towards the fireplace.* HENRIETTA *exits* R.)

BRISBY (*moving to the* R. *of the easy chair* R., *to* GRACE, *heavily*). Ah, Grace, my dear....I can't tell you how sorry....how deeply grieved Claire and I are....how we feel for you.
GRACE. Thank you, Mr Brisby.
BRISBY. There is a terrible mystery here which we must get to the bottom of. Where is Mr Harris ?
DR WADD. Telephoning, I think.
BRISBY. And my wife....does anyone happen to know where she is ? I asked her to wait for me in the sun lounge.
DR WADD. Mr Harris was talking to her a few minutes ago. She's gone to her room, I think.
BRISBY (*surprised*). Mr Harris talking to her ? (*Quickly.*) Do you mean that he was asking her questions ?
DR WADD. I suppose so.
BRISBY (*annoyed*). Quite uncalled for ! I could have answered any enquiries he might wish to make. Gone to her room, you say....
DR WADD. Yes. Grace, better see that girl does her soaking properly. She has a complete belief that if she doesn't follow her doctor's instructions she'll get better.
GRACE. I'll see to it.

(*She goes out up* C.)

MONK. How I should like to be a doctor with all his patients fairly bursting with gratitude for him.
DR WADD (*dryly*). So should I.
MONK. When I was a child....
BRISBY. Not so very long ago.
MONK. Thank you....My mother used to insist on us having a lady doctor....Quite embarrassing.
DR WADD (*lighting a cigarette*). I'm sure you were a very modest young man. (*He offers a cigarette to* MONK.)
MONK. Thanks. (*He takes a cigarette and sits on the stool.*)
DR WADD. It's surprising how one changes as one grows up, isn't it ? (*He crosses to* BRISBY.)
MONK. Thank you. Thank you. As it happens, I haven't.
DR WADD. Changed....or grown up ?
MONK. I pass by that remark in the silence it deserves. But, as I was saying, my lady doctor used to kiss me.
DR WADD. She was indeed a martyr to her profession. (*He pauses.*) Cigarette, Brisby ?

(BRISBY *shakes his head.*)

MONK. It was I who was the martyr. Ever been kissed by a lady doctor ?
DR WADD (*with great emphasis*). I have *not !*
MONK. Quite an experience. Pumice stone, with a flavour of carbolic.

(HARRIS *comes in up* C.).

Ah....my colleague....!

(WADD *goes up to the* L. *arm of settee and sits.*)

BRISBY (*moving up to* HARRIS). I understand you have been asking my wife questions ?

HARRIS. Yes.

BRISBY. You have no right to do any such thing. Were your enquiries official ?

HARRIS. Yes and no.

BRISBY (*angrily*). That is no answer. None at all. You told me that one of your superiors would be in charge of this case. You have no right to commence taking statements in his absence, and in any case I understand a witness has to be present.

HARRIS. I think you misunderstand the situation. The enquiries I made were purely preliminary ; if Mrs Brisby made any statements I should have been unable to take them, officially, until the arrival of the other officers.

BRISBY. In that case there was no excuse for making the enquiries.

HARRIS. I disagree with you, sir. No one who is innocent can have anything to hide....

BRISBY. Good God, sir ! Are you suggesting that my wife has....

DR WADD. Take it easy, Brisby, these things have to be done, you know.

BRISBY (*turns away and moves down to* WADD). If they have to be done, they have to be done properly and in order.

HARRIS (*moving down to* R. *of the easy chair* R.). I am sorry, Mr Brisby, if my speaking to your wife has annoyed you.

BRISBY. It has, definitely, annoyed me.

MONK (*reproachfully*). There, now, Inspector ! You've gone and annoyed Mr Brisby !

BRISBY. I don't need any assistance from you, Mr Monk.

MONK. The soft answer, Mr Brisby. Always the soft answer.

(MRS CORNTONHART *comes in* R. *The men rise.*)

MONK. Enter the private lives of Henry the Eighth !

MRS CORNTONHART (*standing down* R.). Well, have you got any further in your investigations, Mr Hattress ?

HARRIS. Harris, madam. I can't say I've begun yet.

MRS CORNTONHART. Not in a hurry, are you ?

HARRIS. Mr Brisby thinks I'm in too much of one.

MRS CORNTONHART (*with a look of disfavour at* BRISBY). Does he ? Perhaps he has good reason.

BRISBY. Well ! Upon my....(*He moves to the easy chair down* L. *and sits.*)

MONK. Gently, brother, gently. Remember the soft answer.

MRS CORNTONHART (*to* HARRIS). Is it asking too much to enquire whether you have the least idea who committed this crime .... if it was one ?

HARRIS. I think I can answer that.

MRS CORNTONHART. Well ?

HARRIS. At the moment, I haven't the least idea.

MRS CORNTONHART. Got as far as finding any motive ?

HARRIS. No.

MRS CORNTONHART (*scathingly*). Useful sort of officer, you seem to be.

HARRIS. I think I should explain that until the arrival of my superiors from Scotland Yard, I can do no more than ....

MRS CORNTONHART. You'd like to know of a motive—unofficially or not, wouldn't you ? (*She crosses and sits on the settee.*)

HARRIS. Certainly, I should.

MRS CORNTONHART. Very well then. I'll give it to you .....

DR WADD. What ....

BRISBY. What on earth are you saying, Mrs Corntonhart ?

MONK. She's not giving it to *you*, Mr Brisby. Don't go about *looking* for trouble.

HARRIS. If you do know of any motive, it would be of the greatest assistance ....

MRS CORNTONHART. Whether it's a motive or an assistance you can judge for yourself. But I can tell you one thing you don't know.... (*She hesitates.*)

HARRIS. Yes. Mrs Corntonhart. Please go on.

BRISBY. I must refuse ....

HARRIS (*holding up his hand*). Please ....

MRS CORNTONHART. James Ondersley was a blackmailer .... on a pretty large scale, too. That enough to go on with ?

HARRIS. More than enough, Mrs Corntonhart (*thoughtfully*) more than enough.

CURTAIN

SCENE 2.

SCENE.—The same. Five minutes later.

When the CURTAIN *rises* HARRIS *is standing* L. *of the settee and is listening to* MRS CORNTONHART, *who is sitting on the settee.*

(*A cocktail table is now set* L.C. *in front of settee.*)

HARRIS. I take it you're prepared to substantiate that accusation, Mrs Corntonhart .... ?

MRS CORNTONHART (*shortly*). You can take it .... or leave it .... just as you like.

HARRIS. But you could prove the statement .... ?

MRS CORNTONHART. I could, young man, if I wanted to.

HARRIS. Does that mean you don't want to ?

MRS CORNTONHART (*sharply*). Use your brains .... for a change. If I paid four hundred a year for ten years to keep something secret, think I am going to talk about it when the only person who knew it is dead.

HARRIS (*with some little excitement*). You mean .... that you yourself were actually being blackmailed by the late Mr Ondersley .... ?

MRS CORNTONHART. How much of this is going down in that note-book of yours ?

HARRIS. None. You are perfectly at liberty to contradict anything you tell me, later, if you wish .... and I'm making no notes.

MRS CORNTONHART. In that case I will tell you. I've been the victim of James Ondersley's blackmailing for ten years.

HARRIS (*astonished*). May I ask ....

MRS CORNTONHART (*interrupting*). When my husband was alive he did something he was anxious the police should never know about ....

HARRIS. Really ? Go on, please.

MRS CORNTONHART. This man, Ondersley, found out. Tried to blackmail my husband .... Husband died.

HARRIS. Yes.

MRS CORNTONHART. Well, you'd think that would have been enough for Ondersley, wouldn't you ? Oh, no ! Oh, dear me, no ! Very sad Colonel Corntonhart committing suicide. But much sadder for Ondersley to lose his income ....

HARRIS. You don't mean .... ?

MRS CORNTONHART. Yes, I do. Death wouldn't stop *him*. Next thing was, the police'd be informed if I didn't continue the payments after his death.

HARRIS. And you did ?

MRS. CORNTONHART. My good man, I had to.

HARRIS. But if your husband was dead .... ?

MRS CORNTONHART. I was alive, wasn't I .... ? And my daughter.

HARRIS. So you went on paying ?

MRS. CORNTONHART. So I went on paying. What else could I do ?

HARRIS. Nothing, I suppose .... Was it .... was it a considerable sum ?

MRS CORNTONHART. Four hundred a year's a considerable sum .... to me.

HARRIS. And you never thought of going to the police, yourself ?

MRS. CORNTONHART. Thought of it ? Of course I did .... but....

HARRIS. They would have acted against Mr Ondersley, you know, not you.

MRS CORNTONHART. Rubbish ! Whole thing would have had to come to light. Wouldn't have minded it so much myself ....

HARRIS. But your daughter ....

MRS CORNTONHART. Yes.

HARRIS (*slowly*). This throws rather a different light upon Mr. James Ondersley. (*He moves to the stool and sits.*) One thing puzzles me, though.

MRS CORNTONHART. Lots of 'em can do that, for all I care. Told you what you wanted to know. Nothing else you need.

HARRIS. I wasn't going to ask you anything more about what you've just told me. But it's hard to understand how a man of Mr Ondersley's wealth and position—Chairman of Ondersleys and all that—would trouble to put himself into danger by blackmailing. He had enough money to go on with legally, by the look of things.

MRS CORNTONHART. Never heard of Ondersley's other ways of spending money ? You don't keep a yacht .... or run horses .... for nothing, do you ? He was as unlucky as he deserved with his horses. " Lucky Jimmy Ondersley " I don't think.

HARRIS. He lost heavily ?

MRS CORNTONHART. More heavily than even the Chairman of Ondersley's could afford.

HARRIS. I didn't know.

MRS CORNTONHART (*indignantly*). What do ye *do* in Scotland Yard ? Send out summonses for dog licences ? Ondersley's losses are common property.

HARRIS. Sorry .... I hadn't heard of them. I simply knew of him as a business man, in a big way.

MRS CORNTONHART. Big ! But in what way ?

HARRIS. You mean ....

MRS CORNTONHART. What I've told you once. This racket (*with a glance round the room*) and all the rest of it wasn't kept on Ondersley's, plus my four hundred. Others had to pay up.

HARRIS. You know that .... for certain, that he was blackmailing ....

MRS CORNTONHART (*interrupting*). Want it all served on a plate with sauce, don't you ? Stands out a mile what was being done to me was done to others, to keep the show going.

HARRIS. And you connect up this .... murder, if murder it was, with his blackmailing activities.

MRS CORNTONHART. Know a better motive .... ?

HARRIS. No.

MRS CORNTONHART. Do you tell me, if I'd seen a way of finishing him I'd have stopped short of it ?

HARRIS. No .... (*He looks at her.*) No .... I'm sure you wouldn't.

MRS CORNTONHART. Well, then ?

HARRIS (*a thought striking him*). You did, of course.

MRS CORNTONHART. Did what ?

HARRIS. Stop short of it.

MRS CORNTONHART. Very clever, Mr. .... what did you say your name was .... ?

HARRIS. Harris.

MRS CORNTONHART. Very clever. (*She rises and goes to the table above the armchair, takes a cigarette and lights it.*) But strictly, between you and me, you've got to find someone else to tie up in that rope of yours. I didn't poison James Ondersley.

HARRIS. But you think someone else with the same motive as yourself did ?

MRS CORNTONHART. Looks like it, don't it ? I'll give you a few more of my brains to work with. You seem a bit short of your own. (*She moves back to the settee and sits on the* R. *arm.*)

HARRIS. Please do ....

MRS CORNTONHART. Ondersley asked a group of people here for the week-end, didn't he ? Then told them one of 'em had tried to poison him.

HARRIS. Yes.

MRS CORNTONHART. Well .... ?

HARRIS. Well .... ?

MRS CORNTONHART. Dam' slow well to get water out of, you are. Ondersley was blackmailing someone else in this party as well as myself. That party wouldn't play ball. Tried to poison Mr Ondersley.

HARRIS. Yes .... I see ....

MRS CORNTONHART. Mr Ondersley retaliates with this party, threatens not only blackmail now, but attempted murder ....

HARRIS. Yes .... yes .... but....

MRS CORNTONHART (*silencing him in a gesture*). That's why, having made his threat, he left it at that .... Wouldn't say a word till next morning, certain the other one would give in.

HARRIS. And then .... ?

MRS CORNTONHART. And then ! Other one didn't confess .... instead of that, finished off James Ondersley.

HARRIS. But how .... ? He couldn't tamper with the candied peel Ondersley was eating ?

MRS CORNTONHART. Who said he did ? Haven't you any *ideas* ? What about that last whisky and soda before bed ?

HARRIS. What last whisky and soda ?

MRS CORNTONHART. Men always have a last whisky and soda when they get together. Don't you even know *that* ?

HARRIS. I can find out what happened last night at least. (*He rises and presses the bell near the fireplace.*)

MRS CORNTONHART. What are you going to do ?

HARRIS. Ask Mrs Seddons. (*He stands in front of the stool.*)

MRS CORNTONHART. Coming on, you are. Thought of that all by yourself ! (*She crosses down* L. *to the side of the easy chair.*)

(MRS SEDDONS *comes in up* C.)

HARRIS. Sorry to bother you, Mrs Seddons. Just one more thing I wanted to ask you. Did the gentlemen have a whisky and soda last night before going to bed ?

MRS SEDDONS (*coming down between the easy chair and the settee*). Oh, yes, sir.

HARRIS. Where ?

MRS SEDDONS. In the library, sir.

HARRIS. How many glasses ?

MRS SEDDONS. I brought in four, sir.

HARRIS. They've been washed up, of course.

MRS SEDDONS. I should hope so, sir.

HARRIS. They would be ! .... How many glasses were used ?

MRS SEDDONS. All four, sir.

HARRIS (*with a hopeless shrug*). All right, thanks, Mrs Seddons.

MRS SEDDONS. Thank you. (*She goes to the door up* C.)

HARRIS (*moving up to the* R. *corner of the settee ; suddenly*). You weren't there when they were having their whiskies, I suppose ?

MRS SEDDONS. Oh, no, sir.

(MRS SEDDONS *is at the door now up* C.)

HARRIS (*to* MRS CORNTONHART). So there's no way of finding out who poured them out, without asking one of ....

MRS SEDDONS. I beg your pardon, sir.

HARRIS. Yes.

(MRS CORNTONHART *turns her back to the scene, and takes a newspaper from the easy chair down* L.)

MRS SEDDONS. Did I understand you wished to know who poured out the whiskies the gentlemen had ?

HARRIS. You certainly did. You don't know, do you ?

MRS SEDDONS (*coming down a little*). Oh, yes, sir.

HARRIS. Who was it ?

(MRS CORNTONHART *puts down the newspaper abruptly and waits for the answer.*)

MRS SEDDONS. Mr Brisby.

HARRIS (*excitedly*). Are you sure ?

MRS SEDDONS. Quite. Mr Ondersley was writing a note .... for Dr Wadd I think it was, and he asked Mr Brisby to help himself to a whisky and pour out one for him.

HARRIS. Thank you, Mrs Seddons.

(MRS SEDDONS *goes out up* C.)

MRS CORNTONHART (*going to the stool and sitting*). One thing is clear to me.

HARRIS. What's that ?

MRS CORNTONHART. If this mystery's solved, it'll be a couple of women who do it.

HARRIS. I'm grateful for the suggestion. Of course, it's all pure theory. (*He sits on the* R. *arm of the settee.*)

MRS CORNTONHART. Pure theory, my foot! What's Claire Brisby so upset about?

HARRIS (*turning*). Yes .... yes .... She was upset .... But why?

MRS CORNTONHART. If you know that you'll know a lot. Why not ask her.

HARRIS. I can't do that. Her husband objects.

MRS CORNTONHART. Doesn't even that suggest anything?

HARRIS (*rising*). By Jove .... it does ....

(DR WADD *comes in up* C.)

DR WADD (*coming down* R. *of the table above the settee*). Interrupting?

(HARRIS *shakes his head.*)

MRS CORNTONHART (*throwing her cigarette into the fireplace*). Why doesn't the man keep Christian cigarettes? I'll have to get my own from my bedroom. (*She crosses to the door up* C.)

DR WADD. Let me get them for you.

MRS CORNTONHART (*moving to the door*). No thanks .... You have to be careful who you let into your bedroom these days.

(*She goes out up* C.)

DR WADD (*slowly, as the door closes behind her*). I wouldn't really have thought it.

HARRIS. What?

DR WADD. That Mrs Corntonhart has to be careful who she lets into her bedroom. (*He moves to the easy chair* R.) Well, how are you getting on? (*He sits in the easy chair.*)

HARRIS. Unexpectedly well .... Did you have a whisky with Mr Ondersley last night .... in the library?

DR WADD. I did.

HARRIS. Who poured it out? (*He moves to the* L. *of* WADD.)

DR WADD. Why do you ask that?

HARRIS. Never mind for the moment. Who did?

DR WADD. As a matter of fact that's rather curious .... it was poured for me when I came in .... rather too strong. I had to put more soda to it.

HARRIS. So you don't know who actually poured it out?

DR WADD. No. Ondersley, I suppose.

HARRIS. But it might have been, say .... Brisby?

DR WADD. It might have been.

HARRIS. What was Mr Ondersley doing when you came in?

DR WADD. Writing out the address of a fellow who sells springers. I asked him for it .... Why all this?

HARRIS. So, if he was writing at a desk it probably *was* Brisby.

(CLAIRE BRISBY *comes in* R. *followed by* BRISBY. *She crosses to the mantelpiece, gets a cigarette, lights it and then sits in the armchair from down* L.)

DR WADD. Might have been. Why not ask him? Remember that whisky we had last night, Brisby?
BRISBY. What about it?
DR WADD. Harris wants to know who poured it out.
BRISBY (*crossing to the fireplace in front of the stool*). I see no reason for satisfying Mr Harris' curiosity. I have had quite enough of his irregular questioning.
HARRIS. No need to answer .... yet, Mr Brisby, but if you did it might save us a little time when the Inspector arrives. (*He sits on the* L. *of the settee.*)
BRISBY. What *do* you want to know?
HARRIS (*moving nearer to* BRISBY). If it was you poured out the whiskies last night. Mr Ondersley asked you to, didn't he?
BRISBY. Yes.
HARRIS. And did you?
BRISBY. No .... if you want to know, I did not.
HARRIS (*looking at him sharply*). You did not?
BRISBY. No.
HARRIS. Although Mr Ondersley asked you?
BRISBY (*rising and facing him*). Look here, Harris, what the devil are you getting at?
DR WADD (*looking very directly at* BRISBY). I imagine he's trying to get at Ondersley's murderer, Brisby.
BRISBY. Are you suggesting I don't know that?
DR WADD. No. But I'm suggesting you're making it about as hard for him as you can.
BRISBY. I resent that remark.

(MRS SEDDONS *comes in up* C.)

MRS SEDDONS (*to* HARRIS). Excuse me, sir.
HARRIS. Yes, Mrs Seddons.
MRS SEDDONS. It was about those glasses ....
HARRIS. Yes? What about them?
MRS SEDDONS. I didn't know if you'd like to know .... You asked me if they had been washed up ....
HARRIS (*eagerly*). Do you mean they haven't?
MRS SEDDONS. Three of them have, sir, but unfortunately .... one was broken .... that was how Henrietta cut her hand ....
DR WADD (*rising and going round to the* R. *of the armchair*). Have you got the pieces?
MRS SEDDONS. Yes, Doctor.
HARRIS. And they haven't been washed?
MRS SEDDONS. No.
HARRIS. It's very clever of you to have thought of this, Mrs Seddons. I'd like to see those pieces. Will you come, Wadd?
DR WADD. Certainly.
MRS SEDDONS. They're in the maid's pantry .... if you come this way.
D2

HARRIS. Thanks.

(*He follows* MRS SEDDONS *out of the room up* C.)

DR WADD (*as he goes*). I'm sorry you resent anything I've said, Brisby, I did not intend to annoy you.

(WADD *goes out up* C.)

BRISBY (*not very graciously*). Oh, that is all right. (*He sits again on the settee.*) But I have never, in all my life, heard of a more irregular procedure than the way this man is going on. Here we are, seven hours after Ondersley's death has been discovered, and no one has come from Scotland Yard. It is utterly irregular.

CLAIRE. I don't understand why .... why nothing is being done.

BRISBY. It is my belief that this man Harris is trying to handle the case himself for as long as he can in the hope of getting the credit for himself before it is taken out of his hands. I cannot, too, too highly ....

CLAIRE (*interrupting him*). Leonard ....

BRISBY (*surprised*). My dear, *I* was speaking.

CLAIRE. Yes, but I wanted to ask you something.

BRISBY. Well .... what is it ?

CLAIRE. Who .... who do you think sent the poisoned candy ?

BRISBY. My dear Claire .... how should I know ? If I knew that .... there would be no mystery.

CLAIRE. But somebody did. You do think that ?

BRISBY. Undoubtedly.

CLAIRE (*hesitatingly*). Somebody who must have hated James Ondersley.

BRISBY. It was hardly to be described as a friendly act.

CLAIRE (*rising and suddenly going towards the* R. *of settee*). I'm frightened ! .... I'm frightened !

BRISBY. Please calm yourself. There is nothing whatever to be frightened about.

CLAIRE. But there is .... There is ....

BRISBY. And what, may I enquire ?

CLAIRE. I'm frightened that we .... that we may get caught up in this.

BRISBY. That is altogether unreasoning. The publicity that must attend this extraordinary affair will be distressing, no doubt, but beyond that....

CLAIRE. It isn't only the publicity !

BRISBY. What on earth do you mean ?

CLAIRE. Leonard .... I don't know how to say it .... but....

BRISBY (*a little impatiently*). How to say what ? Will you kindly endeavour to explain yourself ?

CLAIRE. Please try and be patient. You remember it was James Ondersley's birthday on the first of June last ....

BRISBY. I don't think I ever knew the date of his birthday. What's that to do with this matter ?

CLAIRE. I bought a box of candied peel from Maxim and Tanders.

BRISBY (*looking up at her*). You did .... ? Well .... ?

CLAIRE. I was going to give it to him for his birthday, then you remember he was away that month .... don't you ?

BRISBY. I remember that he was away, certainly, but I do not at all understand ....

CLAIRE. I intended to give him the box when he came back .... but when I went to look for it .... it was gone.

BRISBY (*angrily*). Gone ? What do you mean by " gone " ?

CLAIRE. It wasn't there .... Somebody must have taken it ....

BRISBY. But this is ridiculous .... You must have put it somewhere else yourself.

CLAIRE. No, no, I'm positive I left it in the wardrobe in my boudoir ....

BRISBY. Then one of the maids must have taken it.

CLAIRE (*moving to the armchair down* L). No .... I don't believe they would. Why should they ? ....

BRISBY. Obviously, no matter where it has gone to, this box of candied peel has nothing to do with the case.

CLAIRE (*turns*). But I must tell Mr Harris .... Mustn't I .... ?

BRISBY (*rising and coming down to her ; angrily*). Are you mad, Claire ? Do you realise what it means if you do ? We shall have detectives searching the house. You will be forced to give evidence .... Even I shall be dragged into it.

CLAIRE (*going up to the settee again*). But where .... where did the box go to .... ?

BRISBY (*roughly*). In heaven's name, how should I know ?

CLAIRE (*agitatedly*). But I must tell the detective ? It wouldn't be honest to keep it back. (*She sits on the settee.*)

BRISBY (*up to the* L. *of her ; angrily*). Heavens above ! What is there dishonest in your buying a box of sweets .... ? You are losing your head. If you tell Harris you will be pushing yourself into the limelight. It would be little short of ruin.

CLAIRE. But I can't .... I can't go on without telling them the box has been stolen, can I .... Why it might be *the* very box .... he was sent.

(MRS CORNTONHART, *smoking a cigarette, comes quietly into the room up* C. BRISBY *has his back to her.*)

BRISBY (*coldly and with emphasis*). You are just being fantastic. You must say nothing whatever about it to anyone. (*Leaning over to her.*) Do you understand ? Nothing whatever ! You may make an infinite amount of mischief if you do.

MRS CORNTONHART. And very good advice, I'm sure .... but what's it all about, eh ?

BRISBY (*turning round, startled*). Mrs Corntonhart .... You're ....

MRS CORNTONHART. Couldn't help hearing that last remark. Well, what's it about, Mr Brisby ?

BRISBY. You are interrupting a private conversation between me and my wife, madam. You have no right whatever ....

MRS CORNTONHART. Shouldn't have private conversations in public places .... if you've got anything to hide. (*She crosses down* L. *near the easy chair.*)

CLAIRE. But Mrs Corntonhart ....

BRISBY (*interrupting her*). That is a most reprehensible statement. You owe my wife an apology.

MRS CORNTONHART (*very rapidly*). Sorry. Beg your pardon. Not at all. Incident closed. What *are* you trying to hide ?

BRISBY. This is unbeatrable.

MRS CORNTONHART. Don't talk like a cuckoo clock !

(MONK *enters* R. *carrying a tray with glasses. He is followed by* LUCY.)

MONK (*a little excitedly*). Behold the new housemaid ! A perfect gem ! Absolutely dependable with the bric-a-brac and the knick-knacks. (*Admiring himself.*) *What* a treasure .... !

LUCY. Put it down carefully ...... Treasure !

MONK (*putting down the tray on the cocktail table in front of the settee with an elegant wave*). There we are ! (*He sends the contents of the tray flying to the floor with a crash.*) Hell ! (*He goes on his hands and knees to retrieve the wreckage.*)

LUCY (*bitterly*). *What* a treasure ! (*She goes down to join him.*)

MRS CORNTONHART. What a bull in a china shop. (*She sits in the armchair.*)

LUCY (*pushing him out of the way*). Let me do it !

MONK (*getting up ruefully and surveying the wreckage*). The bric-a-brac's all bric-a-*broke* now.

LUCY (*putting things back on the tray*). You're lucky. There's only one glass gone.

MONK. That's fine. Everyone can have a drink except (*with a smile at* MRS CORNTONHART) Mrs Correspondence-Course ! ....

(DR WADD *comes in up* C. *with* MR HARRIS *as he is speaking.*)

Hello, Doctor. Sherry ?

DR WADD. No thanks. (*He moves to the* R. *of the table behind the easy chair.*)

MRS CORNTONHART (*to* HARRIS). Got any news for us, Mr Harding ?

HARRIS (*patiently*). *Harris.*

(MONK *sits in the easy chair.*)

MRS CORNTONHART. Your friends from Scotland Yard arrived yet ?

HARRIS. Their car has broken down .... (*He comes down to between the easy chair and the settee.*)

MRS CORNTONHART. Should have taken a hansom.

HARRIS. I expect they'll be here within an hour. (*To* LUCY.) I understand dinner's nearly ready. Perhaps it'd be as well ....

BRISBY (*moving to the down stage end of the cocktail table with great dignity*). Mr Harris.... (*He clears his throat.*) The ineptitude that has been displayed in this case is highly er .... highly .... highly....

MONK. Inept ?

BRISBY. Inept .... Certainly not ! (*Angrily.*) I wish you would let me finish what I was saying.

MRS CORNTONHART. Let your wife begin saying what *she* wants. We might learn something.

BRISBY. Really .... Really, I ptotest. ....

MRS CORNTONHART. Come on, Mrs Brisby. It'll have to come out some time .... Like a bad tooth.

HARRIS. What are you referring to, Mrs Corntonhart ?

BRISBY (*crossing to* HARRIS). I protest .... I protest most emphatically. .... Miss French .... the telephone .... I wish to speak privately.

LUCY. There's a 'phone in the library, Mr. Brisby.

BRISBY (*moving across the room to the door* R). Thank you .... Thank you .... I do not propose to ....

MRS CORNTONHART. Shouldn't let him out of your sight, Mr Harrop, if I were you.

BRISBY (*turning back*). But this is ..... this is intolerable ....

HARRIS. I'm still in the dark about it all, Mr Brisby. You really must not blame me.

BRISBY. Did I ever say, sir, that I blame you for this ? It is for your utter disregard of ....

MRS CORNTONHART (*interrupting*). Don't be led away by all that stuff. (*She rises to her feet and crosses to the* R. *end of the settee.*) If you want to know, I'll tell you what I heard ....

HARRIS. Perhaps you'd better ....

BRISBY. But this is monstrous ....

MRS CORNTONHART. Who's the monster ? I heard him (*she points to* BRISBY) telling his wife—if she told the police something—it would be ruin to him .... (*To* BRISBY.) Deny that if you can.

BRISBY. This is the grossest misrepresentation !

MRS CORNTONHART (*to* CLAIRE). You won't deny it.

CLAIRE. I .... I only ....

HARRIS (*quietly*). If there *is* anything, Mrs Brisby, it would be wiser to tell my superiors from Scotland Yard when they arrive ....

CLAIRE. Yes .... Yes .... I will .... I must ....

BRISBY (*outraged*). Claire .... How dare you take such a step without my ....

(HENRIETTA *has entered,* R., *and he stops speaking.*)

LUCY (*rises to go* R.). Dinner, Henrietta ?

HENRIETTA. Yes, Miss French.

(*She goes out* R.)

LUCY. Dinner is ready .... Shall we ....

MRS CORNTONHART (*making for the door down* R.). We shall .... And there'll be no need to make polite conversation by the look of it.

(*She goes out* R.)

MONK (*rises*). Dinner always comes at just the right time in this house.

DR WADD. Come along, Mrs Brisby .... (*He crosses to* CLAIRE.) Coming, Brisby ?

(CLAIRE *rises slowly to her feet and goes to the door* R. *with* WADD *followed by* BRISBY.)

BRISBY (*very heavily*). If I go to this dinner table, it is solely because it is my duty to protect my wife .... (*He goes out, still talking.*)

MONK (*to* LUCY). Following in the footsteps of the Great Protector, Harris ?

HARRIS. Thank you.

(*He goes out.*)

LUCY. It seems all fantastic .... our sitting down to dinner like this.

MONK. Everything in life is a phantasy .... except hunger .... After you, hostess.

(*He switches off the chandelier. The door down* R. *is open into the dining room.* LUCY *goes out, followed by* MONK, *and the stage is left empty for a short period during which the voices of the guests are clearly and loudly heard. At the end of this period* ONDERSLEY *enters up* C. *He helps himself to sherry and lifts his glass slowly, with a smile, as though in an ironic toast to his guests in the dining room. Then he crosses to the wall brackets and switches them off. The room is lit by firelight, and the light which comes from the dining room.* ONDERSLEY *crosses to the dining room door* R. *and pauses. As he does so the chatter abruptly ceases as the guests at dinner see him. There is a scream and the sound of a breaking glass. He enters the room.*)

CURTAIN

ACT III.

SCENE.—The same, after dinner, the same evening.

When the CURTAIN *rises the room is in darkness except for the light which comes through the open dining room doors and the firelight. Men's voices are heard in the dining room.* LUCY *enters* R. *followed by* CLAIRE *and* MRS CORNTONHART. *She switches on the wall lights, and* MRS SEDDONS *enters* R. *with the coffee which she places on the table in front of the settee.* MRS CORNTONHART *goes to the settee and sits.* CLAIRE *goes to the top of the settee,* L. LUCY *goes to the coffee table and pours out the coffee. The cocktail table is still in the same place, but the pouffe is moved down to the* L. *of the armchair, down* L.

MRS SEDDONS (*standing by the* L. *end of settee*). I think everything's here, Miss French. I suppose the gentlemen will be taking their coffee in here, as usual.

CLAIRE (*who is excited and happy—sits on the stool.*) Gosh ! They'd better. Mrs Seddons, isn't it wonderful about Mr Ondersley ?

MRS SEDDONS (*unmoved*). Wonderful, madam, but when you've lived with a gentleman as long as I've been with Mr Ondersley .... you get accustomed to anything.

CLAIRE. But not to his dying and coming alive again, surely ....

MRS SEDDONS (*cautiously*). I certainly haven't known him do *that* before.

CLAIRE. I don't believe anything would shake you, Mrs Seddons.

MRS SEDDONS. The secret of being a housekeeper in a bachelor's household—if I may say it with respect to Mr Ondersley—is not allowing yourself to be shaken by anything. I hope this isn't too strong, madam. (*She hands coffee to* MRS CORNTONHART.)

MRS CORNTONHART. Stronger the better !

LUCY. The only thing that worries me is, won't there be a lot of talk in the village about this death and resurrection business ?

MRS SEDDONS. No, Miss French, there won't.

CLAIRE. Why not ?

MRS SEDDONS. No one knows.

(LUCY *takes a cup of coffee to* CLAIRE.)

LUCY. But why not ?

MRS SEDDONS. Nobody's been here from the village to find out. It's Sunday.

LUCY. Good Lord, so it is.

CLAIRE. Well, it's a great mercy. It wouldn't quite have done, would it ?

LUCY. No. J. O. almost certainly thought .... wait a moment, though .... Miss Pethington. (*She crosses to the mantelpiece.*) Why, she must have called for her letter. I left it on the mantelpiece. Has Miss Pethington been, Mrs Seddons ?

MRS SEDDONS. I didn't hear of anyone calling, Miss.

LUCY. That's funny. I could have sworn I left it here.

(LUCY *helps herself to some coffee and goes back to the settee and sits.*)

MRS SEDDONS. Now that you mention it, Miss, I think I recollect seeing Miss Pethington this afternoon. Leaving the garden, she was. But I didn't think she had been in the house.

LUCY. Oh, somebody must have given it to her. (*To* CLAIRE.) Mr Ondersley gave her a cheque for something or other she's interested in.

CLAIRE. He's wonderfully generous. Gives an enormous lot away, doesn't he ?

MRS CORNTONHART (*with quite startling suddenness*). Hah !

CLAIRE. I beg your pardon.

MRS CORNTONHART (*with great vigour and directness*). I said " Hah ! "

MRS SEDDONS. Anything else you wanted, Miss ?

LUCY. I don't think so, thanks.

MRS SEDDONS. Then I'll get along. Washing up's a bit slow with Henrietta not able to use her hand.

LUCY. How thoughtless of me. I'll deputise for Henrietta. (*She jumps up.*)

CLAIRE. I'll help, too. (*She rises.*)

MRS CORNTONHART. Like me to scrub the kitchen floor ?

MRS SEDDONS (*apparently paying no attention to her*). It's very kind of you two (*she pauses*) of you *two ladies* (*she glances at* MRS CORNTONHART *now*) but thank you all the same, I'd rather manage on my own.

LUCY. But we'd like to ....

MRS SEDDONS. No, thank you all the same, Miss. I can manage quite easily. Oh, I'm afraid I forgot to mention it. Miss Grace rang up, just before I brought coffee in.

LUCY. Yes ? I left a message for her at Mrs Lambert's.

MRS SEDDONS. She said she'd be along in a few minutes.

LUCY. Thanks, Mrs Seddons. (*She sits down again on the settee.*)

(MRS SEDDONS *goes out* R.)

CLAIRE. It's rather terrific, this waiting, isn't it ?

MRS CORNTONHART. Very amusing ! Seem to have perked up, haven't you ?

CLAIRE. I should think so .... With James Ondersley alive !
LUCY (*rises*). I'm wildly excited to hear what he *is* going to say.
CLAIRE. So am I. Aren't you, Mrs Corntonhart ?
MRS CORNTONHART (*bitterly*). Wildly !
CLAIRE (*getting her own back*). Of course, I forgot .... *You* can't be feeling too comfortable, can you ?
MRS CORNTONHART. What d'ye mean .... eh ?
CLAIRE (*happily*). Well .... You said J. O. was a blackmailer. Isn't that slander, or something ?
MRS CORNTONHART (*sharply*). Who told you that ?
CLAIRE. Mr Monk.
MRS CORNTONHART. Mr Monk !
LUCY. You did say it though, didn't you ? And Dr Wadd heard you, too.
CLAIRE. Somebody's going to get into trouble when J. O. hears about it. Shouldn't like to be that somebody !
MRS CORNTONHART (*going to help herself to some more coffee*). Kind of you. (*She thinks for a moment, then speaks to* LUCY.) What time's that train, did you say ?
LUCY. Nine-fifteen. (*She sits with* CLAIRE *on the stool.*)
MRS CORNTONHART. Got a car for me ?
LUCY. Yes.
MRS CORNTONHART. I'll go now. Tell 'em—send it round. (*She moves* R. *a little.*)
LUCY (*sweetly*). I can't do that, I'm afraid. Grange won't be here till nine.
CLAIRE. But you won't run away, will you ? You're going to face the music, surely ?
LUCY. I'm sure Mr Ondersley would be disappointed.
MRS CORNTONHART. Time he was.
LUCY. But in any case you can't go, I'm afraid, unless you like to walk three miles to the village. (*With great satisfaction.*) It's pouring with rain.
MRS CORNTONHART (*returning to her seat*). Can I get a car from the village ? (*She puts down the coffee on the table at the back of the settee.*)
LUCY. No.
MRS CORNTONHART. Why not ?
LUCY. There isn't one.
MRS CORNTONHART (*to them both, and looking at them with dislike*). Enjoying yourselves, aren't you ?
LUCY *and* CLAIRE (*together*). Yes.
MRS CORNTONHART. Wish you luck of it. (*She rises, takes a cigarette from the table at top of the easy chair* R., *lights it, and returns to the settee.*)

(GRACE *enters up* C. *and moves down between the easy chair and the settee.*)

CLAIRE. Hello, there you are.

GRACE. Hello, you two ! Can you tell me what it all means ?

LUCY. Mrs Corntonhart .... Miss Lenner.

MRS CORNTONHART. Got a shrewd idea, you know very well.

GRACE. How do you do ? Indeed, I don't know anything .... hardly anything. (*She sits on the arm of the settee.*)

MRS CORNTONHART. *Hardly* anything.

LUCY. It's wonderful. Isn't it, Grace ?

GRACE. It's past all wondering. But hasn't J. O. explained yet ?

CLAIRE. Not a word, my dear. Just sat there all through dinner, grinning like a .... well, you know that grin.

GRACE (*feelingly*). Don't I ?

CLAIRE. I'm afraid my husband wasn't too pleased. He asked J.O. direct, and all he said was that he knew *you'd* want to hear the story and he couldn't tell it twice. (*With some little pleasure.*) Leonard *was* annoyed.

MRS CORNTONHART. Every right to be. Brought down to this mad-house for some silly practical joke.

LUCY. I'm sure there's more than a practical joke in all this.

MRS CORNTONHART. Rubbish. Man says he's dead and isn't. If that's not a practical joke, what is ?

LUCY (*slowly*). Well .... I suppose .... if someone said he wasn't dead .... *and he was* !

(MRS CORNTONHART *angrily stubbs out her cigarette.* CLAIRE *looks at* LUCY *in amazement.*)

CLAIRE. In any case, no sensible man would get an Inspector from Scotland Yard, if it wasn't something serious.

MRS CORNTONHART. James Ondersley isn't a sensible man. You've only to look at him to know he couldn't be sane.

GRACE (*quickly*). You've only to look at him to know he couldn't be insane.

MRS CORNTONHART. So that's the way the wind's blowing. Well, I suppose you're wise. Cast thy bread upon the waters, and it'll come back buttered !

GRACE (*moving to the table at the back of the easy chair*). Thanks for the hint.

CLAIRE. I believe you do know something about all this, Grace.

GRACE (*slowly*). I know only one thing .... that it doesn't make any sort of sense .... The funny thing is .... I don't know if you know.

CLAIRE. You're just being tantalising.

(WADD *and* MONK *come in from the dining room,* R. *followed by* BRISBY. MONK *enters first and goes to the upstage end of the fireplace, next to* LUCY. WADD *switches on the chandelier.*)

MONK (*airily*). Conversation piece ! Ladies in Waiting ! A study in feminine curiosity !

CLAIRE (*eagerly*). Have we missed anything ?
DR WADD. Nothing at all. (*He crosses to the easy chair down* L.) Ondersley is obdurate. He must choose his moment.
GRACE. Coffee, you two ? (*She moves down to the cocktail table.*)
MONK. I'm not old enough to take coffee, keeps me awake.
DR WADD. I'm not young enough. (*Sits in the easy chair.*) Keeps me awake, too.
GRACE. Coffee, Mr. Brisby ?
BRISBY. I thank you .... no. (*He sits in the easy chair* R.)
MONK. Why not, Mr Brisby ? Keeps you awake ? Is it coffee .... or conscience ?
BRISBY. I do *not* find that amusing,
MONK. That's your trouble, sir. (*He sits down by* MRS CORNTONHART *on the settee.*) Ah .... Horse and cart ....

(MRS CORNTONHART *gives him a glance which ought to silence him.* GRACE *sits on the pouffe by the* L. *of the easy chair down* L.)

MRS CORNTONHART. Speaking to me ?
MONK. Yes. You look active. Whose character have you been taking away ?

(*Positions now are :* BRISBY *in the armchair* R., MONK *and* MRS CORNTONHART R. *and* L. *on the settee.* LUCY *and* CLAIRE *on the large stool* L., WADD *in the armchair down* R., GRACE *on the pouffe near* WADD.)

MRS CORNTONHART. Not yours. Can't take away what you haven't got.
MONK (*sadly*). Copped it, that time, didn't I ?
LUCY. You deserved it.
MONK. Yes, I suppose I did. I'd got the wrong atmosphere. Third act stuff this is. Tense, taut, and juicy.
BRISBY (*heavily as usual*). I deprecate this way of speaking about a totally unexplained, and lamentable episode.
CLAIRE. Oh, don't worry, Leonard. It's all right now.
BRISBY. My dear .... I think you are forgetting we are expecting a criminal investigation by Scotland Yard officials. This is what Ondersley's so-called sense of humour has let us in for.
MRS CORNTONHART. Skittles !
BRISBY. I beg your pardon ....

(ONDERSLEY *comes in* R.)

MONK. Enter the deceased in excellent health !
ONDERSLEY (*lightly*). And here we all are .... *Now* children ....
MONK } (*together*) { *Now* .... } (*Their inflections are rising.*)
CLAIRE } (*together*) { *Now* ....
LUCY } (*together*) { *Now* ....
ONDERSLEY (*quietly*). *Now* .... Grace. If you'll give your uncle a cup of coffee, he'll tell you a nice bed-time story (*He moves towards the cocktail table.*)

(Grace *rises to get some coffee and afterwards returns to her seat.*)

Mrs Corntonhart. Better hurry up with it. I'm going on the nine-fifteen.

Ondersley (*speaking to* Mrs Corntonhart). We shall be the losers, and the nine-fifteen the gainer.

(Harris *appears in the doorway down* r.)

Ondersley. Come in, Harris. (*He goes to the coffee table.*) Coffee ?

Harris. Thank you.

Ondersley (*pouring out coffee for* Harris). Now, Grace .... So sorry to hear about the Williamsons. (*He offers* Harris *the coffee.*)

Harris (*taking the coffee*). Thanks. (*He sits on the arm of the settee* r.)

Grace. J. O., *do* go on.

Ondersley. Go on ? Oh, with the bed-time story. Well, where shall I begin ?

Brisby (*rising ; in his best style*). The fullest explanation will hardly suffice to make amends for the extraordinary manner in which we have been treated. I must ask why you thought fit to deceive us in this amazing fashion ?

Ondersley (*moving up stage between* Brisby *and the settee*). Hold on, Brisby. This is my show. I'm on the air. (*To* Grace.) Everybody ready ? Right. This is the eight o'clock news, and James Ondersley reading it.

Brisby (*disapprovingly*). This is not a matter for flippancy, Ondersley. You have told us a whole tissue of falsehoods. (*He walks* r. *and up stage towards the door* c. *and back again.*)

Ondersley. As a matter of fact, I haven't ....

Brisby. To begin with, there is the story of your being dead.

Ondersley. *I* didn't tell you that. But, as a matter of fact, I've told you the truth and nothing but the truth. And I'm going to tell you some more. (*Suddenly.*) *Do* sit down, Brisby, you make me nervous, walking about like a bear with corns.

Brisby (*sitting heavily down in the easy chair* r. ; *sarcastically*). Please do not allow *me* to interrupt you.

Ondersley. Thanks. Well .... As I told you before, an attempt was made to poison me. A box of candied peel was deliberately doctored with Tetrasyll. (*He walks up stage and round the table above the easy chair to the* r. *of* Brisby.)

Brisby. You *still* adhere to that story ?

Ondersley. Don't interrupt ! (*Slowly.*) Yes, you must accept it as a fact. (*Conversationally.*) And I strongly suspected it was one of you in this room at the moment, who sent it .... in the deliberate attempt to kill me.

(*There is a pause after he makes that remark.*)

MRS CORNTONHART. D'ye still believe that ?

ONDERSLEY (*very slowly*). I know it to be a fact. (*He looks at* GRACE.) Yes, my dear, I *know* it to be a fact, now.

GRACE. Who would want to do such a thing ?

ONDERSLEY. *You'd* be surprised. (*He moves to the fireplace.*) I was.... I had two possible actions to take, hadn't I ? To go straight to the police ....

BRISBY. That would have been the proper procedure.

ONDERSLEY. Possibly. I hate proper procedures. And it would have been accompanied by a great deal more publicity than would have been welcomed.

MRS CORNTONHART. Can believe that.

ONDERSLEY (*lightly*). Dear lady, you could believe anything pleasant. It comes so natural to you. (*In a more serious tone.*) So I made a list of the people who might benefit in one way or another through my death .... It was a little shocking, the number there were who'd enjoy life more with me out of the way. (*With a smile to* MRS CORNTONHART.) You agree, I am sure. (*He moves again to between* BRISBY *and the settee.*)

MRS CORNTONHART. Not contradicting you.

ONDERSLEY. It seemed all very far-fetched at first. (*His voice grows serious.*) You appreciate, of course, if my list was to help me it had to include everyone who might have a reason (*he looks towards* MONK *as he speaks*) no matter how remote, or unlikely, still a reason. To begin with, there was my friend and partner, Leonard Brisby ....

BRISBY (*getting up*). I protest ....

ONDERSLEY (*quickly*). You do, my dear fellow, far too much. Please sit down. Claire and Miss French just had to be included for the sake of the plan, nothing more.

(BRISBY *sits.*)

CLAIRE. Flattered. Aren't we, Lucy ?

ONDERSLEY. Then, Monk, whose fortune would be made if I wasn't there to turn down his process.

MONK. And the company's fortune.

ONDERSLEY. Perhaps. But, clearly, Monk had to be of the party.

MONK. I wouldn't have missed it for anything.

ONDERSLEY. Glad someone entered into the spirit of the thing. And Monk is an analytical chemist who probably uses quite a lot of Tetrasyll. .... Then Mrs Corntonhart. There really was a reason for her to have snuffed out my little candle. (*He looks at* MRS CORNTONHART.) Wasn't there ?

(MRS CORNTONHART *makes no answer.*)

And then .... Grace .... Grace Lenner. Yes, my ward, living under my roof and all that .... Most unlikely she would have sent the poisoned sweets by post when all she had to do was to replace one box here by another .... That would have made it all the cleverer.

CLAIRE. J. O. .... Are you joking again ?

ONDERSLEY. Indeed, I am not. (*To the others.*) And remember, on my death .... Grace comes in for my money, little as it is.

GRACE. But that isn't true .... I don't.

ONDERSLEY (*quietly*). You do .... now. (*To the others.*) Grace just *had* to be included. Well .... my list was getting on, and I needed an ally .... I couldn't do it all on my own, even with Wadd's most reluctant agreement.

DR WADD. *Most* reluctant.

ONDERSLEY. Then I recollected that none of you .... not even Miss French, knew Mr Blaire .... my secretary at Edinburgh. Even you had never met him, Brisby, had you ?

BRISBY. I had not, but I fail to see what he has to do with this.

ONDERSLEY. Then you'd better meet him now. (*With a wave to* HARRIS.) Mr Blaire .... meet Mr Brisby, my partner in the firm.

HARRIS. How do you do, sir ? (*He rises and bows.*)

(*There is a general movement of astonishment.*)

BRISBY	(*together*).	(*Shocked to the core.*) Do you mean to say ? ....
CLAIRE		J. O., you *monster* !
MRS CORNTONHART		Straight waistcoat's what you need !
LUCY		(*To* HARRIS.) And I've been so polite to you.

BRISBY (*almost speechless*). You mean to say .... You mean to tell me .... that this young man is *not* an officer from Scotland Yard ?

ONDERSLEY. Certainly not, Brisby. Look at his feet ?

BRISBY. This is intolerable ! That one of the firm's employees .... Damn it, Ondersley, are you making all this up ?

ONDERSLEY. Good gracious, no. You won't appreciate that I'm the most truthful of men .... But, if you've any doubts .... Grace, you know Mr Blaire. Is this he ? ....

GRACE (*in a low voice*). Yes, it is.

ONDERSLEY. And Wadd will corroborate ?

DR WADD. Ondersley is correct.

CLAIRE. But what .... why did you ask .... Mr Blaire ?

ONDERSLEY. It was a choice of someone from Scotland Yard, or someone *you'd think* was from Scotland Yard. (*Looking in* CLAIRE's *direction.*) Mrs Corntonhart, for example, is quite glad Mr " Harris " is not Mr Harris the detective.

MRS CORNTONHART (*standing up ; angry*). You're very clever, aren't you, James Ondersley ? But if you think I'm going to put up with this you're mistaken. I'm going ....(*She begins to move towards the door a step or so, as she speaks.*)

ONDERSLEY. Doucement, doucement !

MRS CORNTONHART. Have my luggage sent down to the station. I'm going to walk down sooner than stay in this house.

ONDERSLEY (*significantly*). You won't be asked to stay long. You will be able to go .... and by the nine-fifteen. Blaire, you want to get up to town to-night, don't you ?

HARRIS. If it's all the same to you, sir.

ONDERSLEY. It will suit me very nicely. The car will be here a little before nine. Better slip up and pack your things. I'll deal with this situation.

HARRIS. Very well, sir. (*He moves to the door* C.)

ONDERSLEY. Sit down, Mrs Corntonhart, sit down.

(MRS CORNTONHART *returns to the settee and sits.*)

Oh, Blaire. You know the papers I was working at this afternoon.... when I was .... when I was dead.

HARRIS. Yes.

ONDERSLEY. They're in my bedroom. Put them in a folder and take them with you to town. They ought to be in the office in the morning.

HARRIS. In your bedroom, you said ?

ONDERSLEY. In my bedroom.

(BLAIRE *goes out up* C.)

BRISBY. Ondersley, I think you have done a very wrong thing, a very irregular thing, in bringing this employee of the firm's into a situation of this sort. I do not know if you intend to continue ....

ONDERSLEY. I do. And the first person to be continued with is my friend here, who has to be away by the nine-fifteen. (*He speaks to* MRS CORNTONHART.) You said I was a blackmailer, didn't you .... Any of you believe that ?

CLAIRE. Utterly ridiculous.

LUCY. Good gracious, no.

ONDERSLEY. And you, Monk .... ?

MONK. Pretty pointless question, isn't it ?

ONDERSLEY. You think I make a little, now and then, by a gentle spot of blackmail, Brisby ?

BRISBY. Absurd suggestion ! Just as absurd as all the rest of this.

ONDERSLEY. Thanks for the vote of confidence. It's a pity you're all wrong.

(*They all register surprise.*)

DR WADD (*surprised*). *This* is a new one on me. You are a surprise packet, J. O.

GRACE. What do you mean ?

ONDERSLEY (*pleasantly*). Just what I say. I've been blackmailing Mrs Corntonhart for the last nine years. To the tune of four hundred a year. That right, ma'am ?

Mrs Corntonhart. You ought to know.

Ondersley (*consulting a little note book*). Three thousand four hundred pounds to date, and another two hundred coming in on the first of next month.

Brisby. So she *was* telling the truth.

Ondersley. The truth, that rare stranger in the mouth of Mrs Corntonhart, was in her when she spoke.

Brisby. But, good God ! .... Ondersley ....

Ondersley (*to* Mrs Corntonhart). There you are ! I've confessed. Nothing stands between me and the prison's gaping jaws, except my victim's kindness. Well, Mrs Corntonhart, we're going to call it a day.

Mrs Corntonhart (*in a low voice*). What do you mean ?

Ondersley. No more blackmail .... and no more secret.

Mrs Corntonhart. No .... I'll go on paying you.

Ondersley. Oh, yes, but not me. (*He looks round.*) But this is getting quite a tête-à-tête. Corntonhart, this lady's late husband, was a good fellow .... and a pal of mine. When he was dying, his good wife made his last moments a hell, just as she had made the rest of his life a hell, trying to persuade him to leave all his money to her and none to their daughter—Mrs Corntonhart's own daughter, mark you.

Mrs Corntonhart. What's the use of all this ?

Ondersley. She worried a sick man into his grave to force him to cut that daughter right out of his will .... Corntonhart died .... and the money was left altogether, every halfpenny of it—to his wife. Nothing to the daughter. (*He pauses, looking at* Brisby.)

Brisby. Very lamentable .... Very lamentable, but nothing unusual. Happens every day.

Ondersley. Corntonhart never signed that will. *That's* the trouble. Well, (*to* Mrs Corntonhart) is it true ?

(Mrs Corntonhart *makes no answer.*)

No answer is necessary. Most unfortunately, I found the man who forged the signature.

Brisby. And you didn't notify the police ?

Ondersley. It would have been hurtful to Joan, who is happily married. I drew Mrs Corntonhart's attention to my discovery. She—perhaps not over cordially—agreed to pay me four hundred a year, which I handed on to her daughter, who thinks it is a legacy from her father.

Mrs Corntonhart (*rises ; in a low voice*). Have you done with me now ?

Ondersley. Yes, except to say that the money might as well go direct to Joan now, in the form of capital .... I've a piece of news for you. You haven't troubled to hear before.

Mrs Corntonhart. What is it ?

Ondersley (*with a beaming smile*). Congratulations. You're a grandmother ! .... I think if you made over the capital to that young man .... it is a young man by the way .... our account might be settled.

(HARRIS *enters up* C. *as they are speaking.*)

MRS CORNTONHART (*going to the door*). Did you bring me here to tell me this ?
ONDERSLEY. Not directly. But things turned out so happily ....
MRS CORNTONHART (*in the uttermost bitterness*). It *would* happen with you. "Lucky Jimmy Ondersley," wouldn't it .... A dog gets poisoned, and you get off. You won't get off all the time, as you have this. (*As she goes, she nearly runs into* HARRIS.)
MRS CORNTONHART. Get out of the way, Mr Harris.
HARRIS. Not Harris .... *Blaire.*

(*She goes out up* C. HARRIS *moves down to the settee and sits on the arm* R.)

BRISBY (*astonished*). Do you mean to tell me, Ondersley, you are going to let her go ?
ONDERSLEY. Why not ? (*He moves down* R.)
BRISBY. But .... but .... she's a would-be murderess. (*He comes down to between the settee and the easy chair.*)
ONDERSLEY (*smiling*). At the moment, certainly.
CLAIRE. You can't. If you'd eaten the candied peel she sent ....
ONDERSLEY. But she *didn't* send it.
MONK. What ?
GRACE (*who is obviously distressed*). You've been wonderfully clever, J. O., but are you sure ?
ONDERSLEY. I'm only *too* sure.
LUCY. You mean that you still think someone .... someone in this room sent it ?
ONDERSLEY. Not *think*. I know. We must finish the story now. You agree, Wadd ?
DR WADD (*reluctantly*). Yes .... I suppose so.
ONDERSLEY. Someone sent me poisoned candied peel. That someone was not Mrs Corntonhart. We are agreed on that, aren't we, Blaire ?
HARRIS. Perfectly.
ONDERSLEY. I made a few enquiries at Maxim and Tanders, and I've an idea of a few people who bought candied peel there. Anyone here amongst them ?
CLAIRE. Yes, I did.
ONDERSLEY. Splendid, why shouldn't you ? And ate it all yourself. .... Greedy !
BRISBY (*hastily*). May we stick to the point at issue.
HARRIS (*rising unexpectedly*). This is the point at issue .... (*To* ONDERSLEY.) You'll excuse me, sir.
ONDERSLEY. Certainly. (*He moves to the settee and sits.*) I'd like you to take over. My voice is going.

HARRIS. Mrs Corntonhart overheard *you* (*to* BRISBY), forbidding your wife to tell me something. This was what you wouldn't let her tell me .... wasn't it ?

BRISBY. It .... it .... I .... I'm damned if I see why I should answer that question.

CLAIRE. Well, I think you should now .... now that J. O.'s quite safe. (*To* ONDERSLEY.) I bought a box from Maxim and Tanders, intending to give it to you for your birthday .... You were away, you remember, for nearly two months ; when I came to look for the box it had disappeared.

ONDERSLEY. Why *should* you object to anyone knowing that, Brisby ?

BRISBY (*suavely*). My dear Ondersley, it would have been utterly abominable to me to have been dragged into a public court because of an innocent purchase of my wife.

ONDERSLEY. Perfectly natural, Brisby. Believe me, I entirely sympathise with your point of view.

BRISBY (*apparently a little mollified*). I hope you do, Ondersley. I think you hardly realise how I dislike this sort of extraordinary adventure you appear to enjoy.

ONDERSLEY. I do, Brisby, but the trouble is that Blaire here thinks .... What *is* your theory, Blaire ?

HARRIS. Do you want me to say, sir ?

ONDERSLEY (*nodding*). M'm.

HARRIS (*to* BRISBY). The reason you didn't want your wife to tell us about that box that disappeared was because *that* was the box you put the poison in and sent to Mr Ondersley.

MONK. The cat pounces !

BRISBY (*jumping up*). Good God, Ondersley ! Do you expect me to listen to this insufferable accusation ?

ONDERSLEY (*rising and quietly walking across to him*). Gently, Brisby. Only for a moment longer. All this had to work itself out. Please listen to me. We're nearly there now.

BRISBY. Really, Ondersley, really ! .... This is too much .... (*He sits down again.*)

ONDERSLEY. I told you I knew who tried to murder me .... I had to ask myself, (*slowly*), " What would a man commit murder for ? " (*He pauses after each word.*) Ambition .... money .... hatred .... jealousy .... love.

GRACE (*suddenly*). No, no, J. O. Don't say that .... Don't say that .... please.

ONDERSLEY. My dear, I must .... now .... (*He looks round at the others.*) It's no secret to any of you, that I love Grace Lenner. It was no secret to you, Blaire ?

HARRIS. No.

ONDERSLEY. It was no secret to me that *you* loved her too .... (*Very deliberately.*) You loved her enough to try to commit murder to get her, didn't you ? Well, did you or didn't you ?

(*There is a tense silence before* HARRIS *speaks. He looks round from one to another as though contemplating escape.*)

ONDERSLEY. Well ?

HARRIS (*in a low voice*). So you knew .... (*He checks himself.*)

GRACE } (*together*). { Oh, God .... !
CLAIRE } { So that was it ....

BRISBY (*aghast ; to* HARRIS). You don't deny it ?

HARRIS. I *do* deny it. It's a lie.

GRACE. You're wrong, J. O. You must be wrong.

ONDERSLEY. You're foolish, Blaire. Your only chance is to admit it. (*Slowly.*) You *did* try to poison me, Blaire ?

HARRIS. You've got to prove that .... and you can't.

ONDERSLEY (*very softly*). It was you .... wasn't it ?

HARRIS. I deny it !

ONDERSLEY (*still quietly*). There's your answer, Brisby .... Why didn't I go to the police ? .... Because I couldn't prove anything. It's been clear enough .... but I couldn't prove anything. Grace had been living in Scotland .... She and Blaire were friends .... very good friends. I knew he loved her .... I knew, *he* knew I loved her .... I stood between Blaire and her. (*He crosses to the bell near the fireplace and presses it, then he continues in a low voice.*) The only way to prove my suspicion was to get the guilty man to incriminate himself .... How could I do it ? ....

HARRIS. So *that* was your idea.

ONDERSLEY. Then this fantastic plan jumped into my mind. Why not confide in the very man I suspected.

GRACE. J. O. ....

(ONDERSLEY *stops her with a gesture.*)

ONDERSLEY. I tried it .... I told Blaire I suspected various people .... absurd people. Then I made the suggestion that he would impersonate a man from Scotland Yard and help me to discover the guilty man.

BRISBY. Absurd !

ONDERSLEY (*quickly*). Precisely .... So absurd that no one would have dreamed of agreeing to my suggestion (*with a sudden vigour*) *except the one man who had everything to gain by fastening the suspicion on someone else's shoulders.* When Blaire accepted .... I *knew* then who my man was .... But I still couldn't prove it ....

HARRIS (*with hatred in his voice*). And you can't now.

ONDERSLEY (*softly again, moving well down* R.). Perhaps I can't .... Perhaps I can .... I don't know yet. But, you see, Brisby, I had to give my man enough rope. To accuse you, on no evidence whatever, was a further evidence of guilt. But I still wanted *proof.*

GRACE (*coming up to* ONDERSLEY). J. O. .... Need you go any further ? If you know .... isn't it enough ? For .... my sake ....

ONDERSLEY. Won't you leave it to me? Am I likely to be unmerciful to anyone who did what he did for you?

(MRS SEDDONS *comes in up* C. *She carries* BLAIRE'S *suitcase in her hand. She puts down the case just inside the door.*)

ONDERSLEY. Thanks, Mrs Seddons .... That's all ....

(MRS SEDDONS *goes out up* C. ONDERSLEY *waits till she has gone before he speaks.*)

ONDERSLEY (*speaking quietly as he crosses to the suitcase up* C.) But, if I've guessed right .... the *proof* is in this suitcase. (*He brings the suitcase down stage* R. *He tries the lock.*) Keys, Blaire, keys.
HARRIS (*moving to take the suitcase*). You've no right to touch my property .... You proved nothing ....
ONDERSLEY (*quietly*). Keys .... or .... not?
HARRIS (*handing him the keys*). You're clever..... Mr Ondersley. Cleverer than I thought.
ONDERSLEY (*opening the case*). I am right, then. (*To the others.*) There was one bait, I thought I might work. The remains of the poisoned candied peel was in my bedroom. Blaire knew it was there. It was to his interest to get it away. That's why I sent him upstairs—alone to my bedroom .... To give him that opportunity .... and here .... of course, is the box. (*He takes it out of the suitcase.*)
HARRIS. All right .... you've got me. What's the next move? The local P.C.?
GRACE (*moving towards* ONDERSLEY). Can you .... do .... one very .... big thing for me .... J. O.?
ONDERSLEY (*to her*). I'm going to do just what you'd want me to. (*He looks at his wrist watch. To* BLAIRE.) It's ten to nine. The car will be waiting now .... and the train goes at nine-fifteen .... You'd better get off, immediately.
HARRIS (*quietly*). You mean you're not going to .... (*He moves rapidly to the suitcase and begins to close it.*)
HARRIS. What?
ONDERSLEY (*very slowly indeed*). There's one thing you're forgetting, Blaire. (*He slowly hands* HARRIS *the box of candied peel.*)

(HARRIS *takes it, looks at it, then at* ONDERSLEY *as though about to speak. Then, in silence, he takes the box, and goes out up* C. *without looking back. There is a moment's silence after he goes.*)

MONK (*giving a long slow whistle*). I hope he'll share the stuff with Mrs Corstalk!
DR WADD. Well, you've pulled it off! .... I didn't believe you could.
ONDERSLEY (*to* GRACE). I hope I have .... without hurting .... anyone.

GRACE. Thank you, J. O. .... It was .... a fine thing to do.
BRISBY (*standing up*). I .... really .... I do not know what to say ....
CLAIRE (*rising and going to* BRISBY ; *vigorously*). Then don't say it, Leonard, you've said quite enough.
BRISBY (*astonished*). Really .... Really .... Claire !
MONK. What I'd like to know is what happened to that box of candied peel of yours, Mrs Brisby.
CLAIRE. So should I.
BRISBY (*much embarrassed*). Well .... as a matter of fact .... if you must know ....
MONK. We must !
BRISBY (*shamefacedly*). I'm rather fond of candied peel myself.
ONDERSLEY (*laughing*). Another addict !
CLAIRE. Why on earth didn't you tell me ?

(HENRIETTA *enters* R.)

HENRIETTA. Miss Pethington.

(*There is a commotion as* MISS PETHINGTON *rushes on* R. *She carries something carefully concealed from the audience in a large hand-bag. She is nearly inarticulate. Those still sitting now rise.*)

MISS PETHINGTON. Dear....dear....Mr Ondersley ! (*Moving to* L. *of* ONDERSLEY.) Your cheque. Such generosity. It's gigan .... it's enorm .... It's *ginenormous* !
ONDERSLEY (*retreating away from* MISS PETHINGTON *and moving towards* GRACE.) Not at all.
MISS PETHINGTON. I fear I will give annoyance .... but I wondered if I might ....
ONDERSLEY. Might what ?
MISS PETHINGTON. If I might bring you .... a little gift. (*She is struggling with the bag as she speaks, and now thrusts the box into* ONDERSLEY's *hands.*)
MISS PETHINGTON. Just a little box of your own dear Candied Peel.

QUICK CURTAIN.

FURNITURE AND PROPERTY PLOT

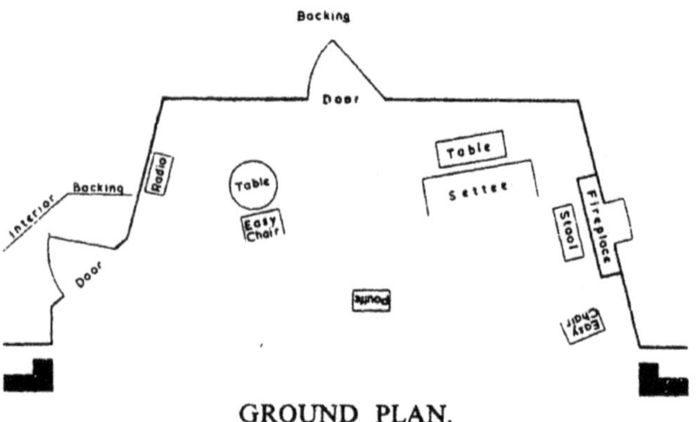

GROUND PLAN.

ACT I. SCENE 1.

Radio.		
Chair.		
2 Easy Chairs.		
Circular Table.	*On it :*	Vase of flowers, ashtray and box of candied peel.
Table.	*On it :*	Bottle of gin, decanter of sherry, cocktail shaker, telephone, a few glasses.
Settee.	*On it :*	Book.
Stool.		
Pouffe.		

Box of cigarettes, matches and clock on mantelpiece.

Personal—

Letters (LUCY).

Tray of drinks (HENRIETTA).

SCENE 2.

Set same as Scene 1.

Sunday papers on circular table and easy chairs.

Personal—

Sunday Pictorial (MRS. SEDDONS).

Notebook (LUCY).

ACT II. SCENE 1.

Set same as previous act.
Letter on mantelpiece.

Personal—
Magnifying glass (MONK).
Cigarette case (HARRIS).
Cigarette case (WADD).

SCENE 2.

Set as before with the addition of a cocktail table in front of the settee.

Personal—
Tray of glasses (MONK).

ACT III.

Set as in last scene except that the pouffe has now been moved to the left of the easy chair down L.
Coffee, etc.

Personal—
Cigarette case (MRS CORNTONHART).
Suitcase (MRS SEDDONS). *In it:* Second box of candied peel.
Keys (HARRIS).
Third box of candied peel (MISS PETHINGTON).

NOTE: The three candied peel boxes should be brightly and conspicuously decorated and identical.

MADE AND PRINTED IN GREAT BRITAIN BY
LATIMER TREND & COMPANY LTD PLYMOUTH
MADE IN ENGLAND

Milton Keynes UK
Ingram Content Group UK Ltd.
UKHW021859080124
435668UK00038B/607